KUNG-FU
MONTHLY

THE ARCHIVE SERIES

THE UNBEATABLE BRUCE LEE

BY THE EDITORS OF
KUNG-FU MONTHLY

COMPILED AND EDITED BY
CARL FOX

PIT WHEEL PRESS
BARNSLEY

Published by
PIT WHEEL PRESS LIMITED
www.pitwheelpress.com

Copyright © 2023 Pit Wheel Press Limited. All Right Reserved. No part of this book may be reproduced, scanned or distributed in any printed or electronic form without permission.

THE UNBEATABLE BRUCE LEE

Copyright © 1978 by H. Bunch Associates Ltd. (except where copyright on certain photographic material already exists). This publication or any parts thereof may not be reproduced in any form whatsoever without permission in writing from the copyright proprietor.

A Pit Wheel Press edition, published by special arrangement with Dennis Publishing, London.

First Printing 1978
Revised Edition 2023

Printed in the United Kingdom
ISBN 978-1-915414-13-7

"All the time, people come up and say, 'Hey Bruce, are you really that good?' I say, 'Well, if I tell you I'm good, probably you will say that I'm boasting. But if I tell you I'm not good, you'll know I'm lying."

Bruce Lee

ACKNOWLEDGEMENTS

I would like to thank the following people for their help and participation in the making of this book:

James Bishop
Andrew Kimura
John Little

John Overall
Carlotta Serantoni
Andrew Staton

Special Thanks
Bey Logan

CREDITS

Original 1978 Edition

PHOTO CREDITS

Golden Harvest Films, Warner Bros Films & Chester Maydole

The Kung-Fu Monthly Archive Series

Research, Editing, Layout & Design
Carl Fox

Editorial Assistance
George Fox

Photograph Acknowlegements
Kung-Fu Monthly & Carl Fox

Kung-Fu Monthly Collage Image
Copyright © 2023 Carl Fox

KUNG-FU MONTHLY

THE ARCHIVE SERIES
THE UNBEATABLE BRUCE LEE

CHAPTERS

	ABOUT THE KFM ARCHIVE SERIES	11
	FOREWORD BY BEY LOGAN	15
	INTRODUCTION (2023) **THE STORY OF THE MAYDOLE PHOTOS**	21
	INTRODUCTION (1977) **AUTHOR'S NOTE**	27
01	**ACTOR, SHOWMAN OR** **MARTIAL ARSTIST?**	31
02	**FROM EMPTY HAND** **TO INTERCEPTING FIST**	53
03	**JEET KUNE DO:** **THE ECLECTIC SYSTEM**	73
04	**JEET KUNE DO:** **THE WAY FORWARD**	113

KUNG-FU
MONTHLY

THE ARCHIVE SERIES
ABOUT THE SERIES

Kung-Fu Monthly is a name synonymous with Bruce Lee, not only in the United Kingdom but throughout the world. It is a legend in its own right and a brand immediately recognisable by not only the font but also the famous "flying man" logo.

The popularity of the magazine at the peak of the Kung Fu Craze in the 1970s was unrivalled and its success was almost entirely down to pure luck.

Legend has it that *Kung-Fu Monthly* began life as a gamble by underground comic book publisher Felix Dennis after questioning a queue of kids outside a Soho cinema, waiting to see *Enter the Dragon* in early 1974. On paper, the idea seemed to serve the then-current trend of Bruce Lee and was deemed to have a shelf life of three to six months but a year after its launch, *Kung-Fu Monthly* had become the biggest-selling Bruce Lee magazine in the world.

After the demise of the Official Bruce Lee Fan Club in 1976, *Kung-Fu Monthly* launched their own. The KFM Bruce Lee Society ran for thirty quarterly newsletters from 1976 to 1983 and at the time of closing, had seen over five thousand eager Bruce Lee fans become members throughout its tenure, with the formidable Pam Hadden at the forefront throughout its seven active years.

Kung-Fu Monthly and The Bruce Lee Society were jointly responsible for the UK's first Bruce Lee Convention held on May 19th 1979 and the first Bruce Lee Film Festival held on December 1st 1979.

Kung-Fu Monthly and later *Personal Computer World*, had turned H. Bunch Associates from an underground publisher on the verge of bankruptcy to a publishing powerhouse, eventually becoming Dennis Publishing, named after its founder, Felix Dennis.

That leads us to today.

In February 2021, I approached Dennis Publishing with an idea for a project that I'd thought of doing for many years - scan, convert, edit and compile all seventy-nine issues of the iconic *Kung-Fu Monthly* magazine into book form, in order to present it to a new audience, as well as preserve its place in history.

It was the longest-running dedicated Bruce Lee magazine of its kind anywhere in the world (by frequency and circulation) and I wanted to pay homage to that. Such was its success and popularity that it was licensed throughout the world; in fourteen countries and in eleven languages. That doesn't even take into account the non-official bootlegs which appeared in China and Turkey. Nothing has matched it before or since. It truly has stood the test of time and having done so, has reached legendary status.

Kung-Fu Monthly is a snapshot of a time long gone; a time which the original fans remember with fondness and a time which new fans will hopefully discover.

The *Kung-Fu Monthly Archive Series* is dedicated to Felix Dennis and everyone associated with the magazine; not just the staff but also the fans, who would buy copies of the magazines in their millions over its lifetime and help cement the publication's place in British Pop Culture history.

Special thanks must also go to Carlotta Serantoni at Dennis Publishing for her assistance in allowing this project to go ahead.

Carl Fox
February 2022

KUNG-FU
MONTHLY

THE ARCHIVE SERIES
THE UNBEATABLE BRUCE LEE

FOREWORD

THE UNBEATABLE BRUCE LEE

To think we can all now agree that, besides being 'Unbeatable,' Bruce Lee is proving to be 'Eternal.' It seems to me a wonderful miracle that The Little Dragon seems even more popular and relevant and illuminated now, all these decades after the founding of 'Kung Fu Monthly' magazine and the publication of the original edition of this book.

When I first started writing for KFM, I suspected that the audience for Bruce Lee would slowly dwindle to a hard core fan base, and that Kung Fu cinema might yield other stars who might replace Bruce, the way Elvis was eventually superseded in the rock world. And, boy, did I get that one wrong! Year by year, Bruce has out-grown all qualifications. First he was the world's most famous martial arts star, then the most famous Chinese person, now the most potent pop culture icon ever. The only possible next step is to see what the outerspace aliens make of Lee when they land...

I felt like I had entered a strange, new world when I first ventured into the hallowed halls of Bunch Books. As an adventurous 20 year old, I had already undertaken a pilgrimage to Hong Kong to walk in the footsteps of the Dragon. On my return, I sent a long letter to Kung Fu Monthly describing my odyssey. This was actually published as an article in the magazine. The late Frank Zappa once observed that "most rock journalism is people who can't write, interviewing people who can't talk, for people who can't read." The same was generally true of martial arts magazines, so I guess it was no surprise that the latest, and last, KFM editor, Colin James, reached out to me about supplying them with more material.

I was just a wide-eyed guy from the provinces (Peterborough!). In my imagination, the Bunch Books HQ on Rathbone Place would be like the London branch of Shaolin Temple. As it turned out, the staff would have fit in better at Woodstock than Wudang. Beads, beards and tie-die were the order of the day. The air was redolent with incense and sundry other substances. I remember a Friday evening when everyone was on edge as they waited for an illicit delivery from a Special Friend.

The first time I visited the Bunch Book offices, the amiable Colin James took me to the pub at lunchtime. I blithely told one of his female colleagues that I didn't drink, smoke or take drugs. She looked me up and down in bewilderment. "What's wrong with you?" What, indeed... Colin, by the way, was always remarkably patient and kind to someone who must have seemed to him as naïve and gauche as I did.

My biggest disappointment was that no-one at KFM trained in martial arts, not even that black guy who modeled the yellow-and-black cat suit! Colin had worked out with a Camden based Kung Fu clown named Dave Lea, and, to my detriment, I ended up training with him, too. Despite the general vague hippie-ness and lack of martial experience on the part of the editorial staff, some incredible work somehow still got done. When you consider that there was no Internet, that no-one spoke Chinese (some of them were barely coherent in English...), few had travelled in Asia... And yet here is 'The Unbeatable Bruce Lee', with its apt quotes from Chuang Tsu and Lao Tse, the detailed account of the martial traditions that led us to Bruce Lee and Jeet Kune Do, including insights into Lee's Wing Chun teacher, Ip Man, the precise captions to the photos of Bruce and Dan Inosanto, demonstrating for Chester Maydole's camera on a Malibu beach...

This was a really ground breaking work, laying the foundations for Matt Polly to write Bruce Lee: A Life and myself Bruce Lee and I. All these years after The Unbeatable Bruce Lee, there are still so many unseen images and unknown facts and even a few film clips...

The Eternal Bruce Lee, indeed!

Looking at the book today, it brings back happy memories of my own Kung-Fu Monthly experiences, and how they informed the paths my life would take. I first read about Hong Kong in the Bunch Books publications, and have now lived in the city for thirty years. I heard about Lee's lost Game of Death footage in the pages of Kung Fu Monthly, and later had the honour of locating it in a Chinese film company archive. I learned kung fu and Chinese and made films with the likes of Jackie Chan and Sammo Hung, and it all started when I read and wrote for KFM.

My deepest wish today is that someone as young now as I was then will read these new editions, prepared by my old friend, the tireless Carl Fox, and be inspired, as I was, to fulfill their own bright destiny!

Bey Logan
Hong Kong 2022

Bey Logan is a writer, film maker and producer from Peterborough, England. Starting out his writing career with *Kung-Fu Monthly*, he progressed on to the magazines *Combat* and *Impact*, before heading to South East Asia in the 1990s to fulfil a dream and work in the Hong Kong film industry. Whilst in Hong Kong, he worked for media giant Media Asia after their acquisition of Raymond Chow's Golden Harvest and its back catalogue. It was during his time at Media Asia that he worked on multiple film projects including *Gen X Cops*, *Twins Effect* and several Jackie Chan movies. He was also responsible for unearthing Bruce Lee's long-lost footage for his final uncompleted 1972 movie, *The Game of Death*, which was eventually used in the John Little documentary, *Bruce Lee: A Warrior's Journey* and the Japanese company Artport's film, *Bruce Lee in G.O.D.*

After Media Asia, Logan began providing audio commentaries for martial arts orientated DVDs released by Medusa Communications' sub-label Hong Kong Legends in the United Kingdom. His audio commentary work brought him to the attention of Hollywood film mogul Harvey Weinstein, who employed Logan to head up the Hong Kong-inspired DVD label Dragon Dynasty for his newly created Weinstein Company, ultimately becoming the parent company's Asian Vice President.

Logan released his memoir *Bruce Lee and I* in 2018 and still resides in Hong Kong, where he runs a successful martial arts club and the Asian film memorabilia company, Reel East.

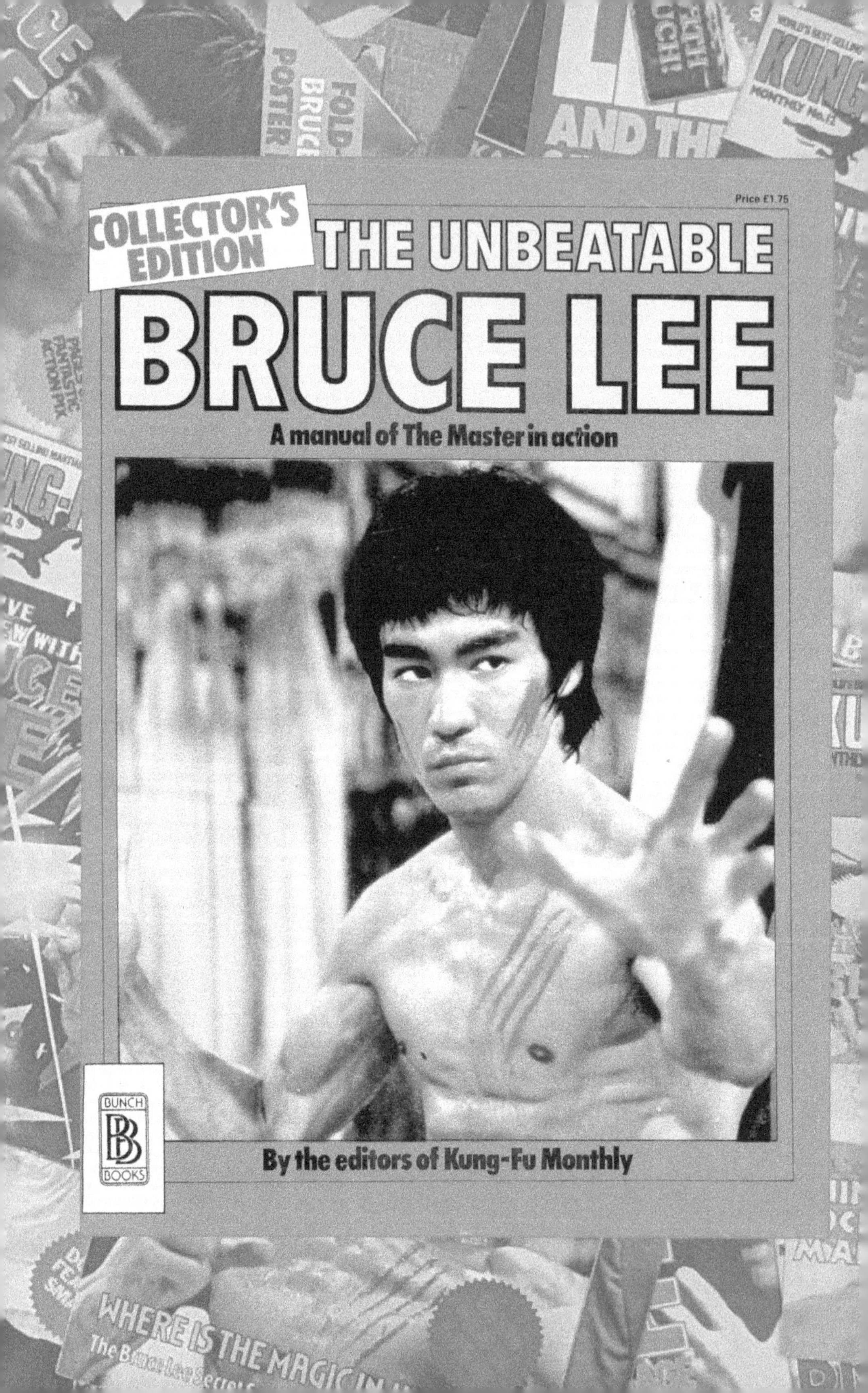

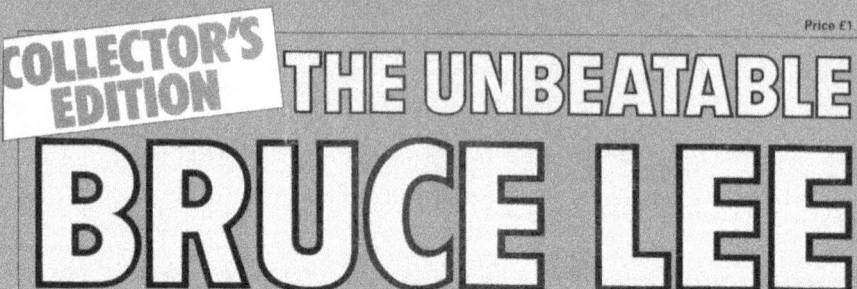

Price £1.75

COLLECTOR'S EDITION

THE UNBEATABLE BRUCE LEE

A manual of The Master in action

BUNCH BOOKS

By the editors of Kung-Fu Monthly

THE UNBEATABLE BRUCE LEE

In 1965, a twenty five year old Bruce Lee has been in the USA for six years, having been sent there from Hong Kong by his father in 1959 after repeatedly getting into fights. After setting up his Jun Fan Gung Fu school, Lee has started attracting famous students such as celebrity hairstylist Jay Sebring.

One of Sebring's clients was William Dozier, the producer of the popular TV show *Batman*, based on the comic book of the same name. Sebring commented to Dozier that he should check out Lee at a local martial arts tournament being held by Ed Parker in Long Beach, California. On 12th June 1965, Bruce Lee walked into the studios of Twentieth Century Fox to participate in a screen test for a new series being developed by Dozier entitled *Number One Son*, about the son of Charlie Chan, the popular fictional Chinese-American detective from several novels and movies from the 1940s and 50s.

Just over two months before the screen test, Lee had become a father to Brandon, the first child between his wife Linda and himself. The director of the screen test tells Lee that he understands he just had a baby boy and asked if he has lost any sleep recently, to which Lee replies, "Three nights!" Unfortunately for Lee at the time, *Number One Son* was never made. When asked six years later by Canadian broadcaster Pierre Berton if it has been made, Lee replied, "No. They were going to make it into a new Chinese James Bond type of a thing. Now that, you know, the old man Chan is dead. Charlie is dead, and his son is carrying on." After missing out on *Number One Son*, Lee returned to teaching martial arts.

A year after the Number One Son screen test, William Dozier was developing a new TV series based on the comic book *The Green Hornet*. Success with another comic book TV series *Batman*, Dozier attempted to cash in on that success by bringing *The Green Hornet* to the small screen. Having already been a hit on radio, *The Green Hornet* was the perfect candidate for the TV treatment and although Dozier didn't have an actor in mind for the lead role of Britt Reid, he knew exactly who he wanted for his Kung Fu fighting chauffeur Kato – Bruce Lee. The role of Kato was actually cast before that of Britt Reid/The Green Hornet as evidenced in several Green Hornet screen tests, where Lee's Kato is seen reading lines with several potential Green Hornets. Eventually, Van Wiiliams was cast in the lead role and confirmed the casting timeline. "I think Bruce was already gotten when I was brought on board," remembered Van Williams. "They still hadn't got The Green Hornet but they had got Kato. I don't think I met Bruce until the press party. Adam West introduced us both and we were there and it was the first time I'd met Bruce and we didn't really have much time to sit down and talk or anything else. He was really a very personal guy." Lee later joked on the reason behind his casting, "I was the only Chinese man in California who could pronounce, 'Britt Reid.'" Van Williams commented in a 1992 interview how Bruce would sometimes struggle with pronouniation, "His biggest problem was that he had a very thick Chinese accent that was very hard to understand and a lot of the lines he read a lot of the people just couldn't understand. So slowly but surely they took a lot of his lines away to the point where it was that he mostly did action stuff and whatever." Lee wasn't entirely happy with his performance in *The Green Hornet* as he told Pierre Berton in 1971, "I did a really terrible job in that, I have to say."

The first episode of *The Green Hornet* was aired on US TV on 9th September 1966. As a pre-planned advertisement, *The Green Hornet* and Kato would make a cameo appearance in *The Spell of Tut*, the ninth episode in the second season of *Batman* which aired on

28th September 1966.

The Green Hornet was a moderate success, though not as successful as William Dozier's other series, *Batman*. In order to increase ratings, it was decided to write some more episodes where the worlds of *Batman* and *The Green Hornet* would join together. *A Piece of the Action* and *Batman's Satisfaction* initially had the duos facing off against each other before joining forces to fight crime.

With Lee now a TV star, the studios had photographers take various publicity shots on and off set; one of those photographers being Chester Maydole.

Chester Maydole was born in 1923 moved to Los Angeles in 1947 after the Second World War in order to pursue a career in the arts. He became interested in photography while visiting a film set, he became interested in photography and began to photograph his neighbours, one of those being Clint Eastwood. In his later career, he began taking portfolio pictures for actors and models. Maydole built up a strong working relationship with actor Steve McQueen as well as photographing actresses Sally Field, Mia Farrow, Raquel Welch and Sharon Tate.

The American Jazz Pianist Les McCann wrote of Maydole, "I think of Chester as my early technique teacher for photography because when I was working in Hollywood, I would go up to his house (each night, after I got out of work) and we'd meet in his darkroom after hours. Over a period of a year or two, I would watch him. It was fantastic. I did my own developing, my own printing, and I learned it all from him. He was a great photographer as well. He took all those cowboy pictures of me."

As stated in *The Secret Art of Bruce Lee*, "At that time, Maydole was working as a 'photographer to the stars,' taking assignments from major film and television studios in Hollywood who needed publicity shots of their actors and actresses."

Maydole recalled, "I'd done some shots of *Batman*, which was very successful at that time, and I was asked by the company to take pictures of Bruce Lee and Van Williams. They were for the fan magazines as I recall."

Maydole photographed Lee in four sessions at four separate locations - Portuguese Bend in South Los Angeles, Lee's apartment in West Los Angeles, Malibu Beach, and Batman star Adam West's beach house in Palos Verdes.

Maydole found Lee extremely easy to work with and very enthusiastic about his new career and was eager to help in any way. "He'd done pictures in Hong Kong before, but I suppose he was making a lot more money now and it must have been quite a thing, a half-hour show which might run for a long time. It didn't, of course, but he wasn't to know that." During the shooting session, both Lee and Maydole enjoyed their professional relationship and they quickly became friends.

"He was a terrific guy," recalled Maydole. "I liked him very much. He was smart - not Hollywood smart, but he really knew his stuff. He was a very natural and down-to-earth sort of person. He didn't take much part in the usual Hollywood goings on; he was more interested in his martial arts. He was a very spiritual person and I know he meditated a lot. After all, Kung Fu is a very heavy thing, especially if you are Chinese and you have all that tradition behind you. It sort of becomes a religion. Yet it's a funny thing that, although Bruce went in for the whole thing, he taught just the opposite. He taught that people don't have to follow ritual. He taught you shouldn't be bound - you should be free."

Maydole remembered Lee as being obsessed with martial arts. He said he was always exercising, constantly performing impromptu movements and the only time he was still, was when he was engrossed in a book from his enormous library.

"I can't say enough about his Kung Fu and his teachings," said Maydole. "I had great respect for him. He had probably the most perfect body I have ever seen. He was small - perhaps 140 pounds - but his physique was most unusual, especially for a Chinese. He worked on it all the time. He was very particular about what he ate. He ate a lot of Chinese food, naturally enough, cooked specially for him by one or two of the Chinese restaurants in Chinatown. I remember how he would sit there eating this special food with all his students around him, holding court."

With his TV career going well, it wasn't long before Lee considered resuming his martial arts career and after looking around the city for a suitable place, he opened a Kung Fu school in Chinatown. Maydole recalled Lee's decision causing waves within the community. "Nobody had ever taught Kung Fu here before. Several top Karate black belts such as Danny Inosanto went over to Bruce and there was a lot of jealousy among the Karate people who said that Kung Fu didn't mean anything. Bruce challenged them on several occasions, but nothing ever came of it. I suppose they knew in their hearts how good he was."

Despite their friendship, Maydole wasn't overly convinced of the self-defence aspect of Lee's martial arts and was concerned about its potentially violent potential. What concerned him more was Lee's deadly expertise in the art. "Bruce had this big wooden dummy which he would use, and once he showed me 52 ways of kicking it. By kicking on a certain place you could blind a person, cripple him, kill him - whatever you chose. And Bruce, with his big toe, he could kick in any one of those 52 places. He was always wearing bare feet or ballet shoes so he could use his toe more freely. His big toe was a lethal weapon. He could kick you with it on the chin from any direction without warning."

In one photography session, Lee and his student Dan Inosanto met with Maydole at *Batman* star Adam West's beach house in Palos Verdes, as confirmed by Inosanto several years later. There is a possibility that some of the photographs – especially the ones taken near West's beach house – were taken by Maydole for a proposed martial arts book collaboration between Lee and West to take advantage of their success on *The Green Hornet* and *Batman* respectively.

Although he never fully trained with him, Maydole was immensely impressed with Lee's skills and soon realised that they would look good on film. The result of that are the photographs in firstly, *The Secret Art of Bruce Lee* and then shortly afterwards, *The Unbeatable Bruce Lee*. "They were taken," recalled Maydole, "just for the hell of it. I thought that with a little pushing, I could sell some of them to a Karate magazine, and so the first of four sessions was set up." On Malibu Beach, Lee and his pupil, Dan Inosanto, ran through a series of attacks and defences in front of Chester Maydole's lens.

Other photographs were taken in Lee's Los Angeles apartment and depict some of Lee's training methods and equipment, plus a section of his vast martial arts library and weapons collection. They represent a small glimpse of Lee the family man realising his dream on the cusp of stardom.

"Bruce was very proud of his wife and young son Brandon," remembered Maydole. "His other child was born after we lost contact with each other. Linda was very quiet. She never said a word which made her rather hard to get to know. Maybe she had decided to take a backseat to Bruce because he was the star. She was a martial artist herself though. And Brandon should be very good at Kung Fu when he grows up, too. Even at that age he was learning."

Unfortunately, Maydole never sold the photographs he took of Lee but his photography career continued upwards and he found himself very much in demand, photographing celebrities such as Farah Fawcett and Lee's old student Steve McQueen. Due to time constraints, they lost contact with each other, although Lee often contacted Maydole to discuss the book project in which he intended to use the photographer's photographs as illustrations. With Maydole tied up travelling the world with work, Lee stopped calling him. "It was just circumstances," recalled Maydole sadly. "Both of us were trying to make a living and, of course, I'm really sorry I didn't do the book."

Having not been used, the photographs that Maydole took were stored away. "I stuck them in my dead picture file and forgot about them," said Maydole. "Then recently my agent mentioned he was after pictures of Bruce Lee. I said I had lots of shots of Bruce doing Kung Fu. And that was that."

After being out of print for over forty years, and with permission from Dennis Publishing, *The Unbeatable Bruce Lee* has been re-released for not only Lee's fans, but also for historical preservation and education of future generations.

Carl Fox
June 2022

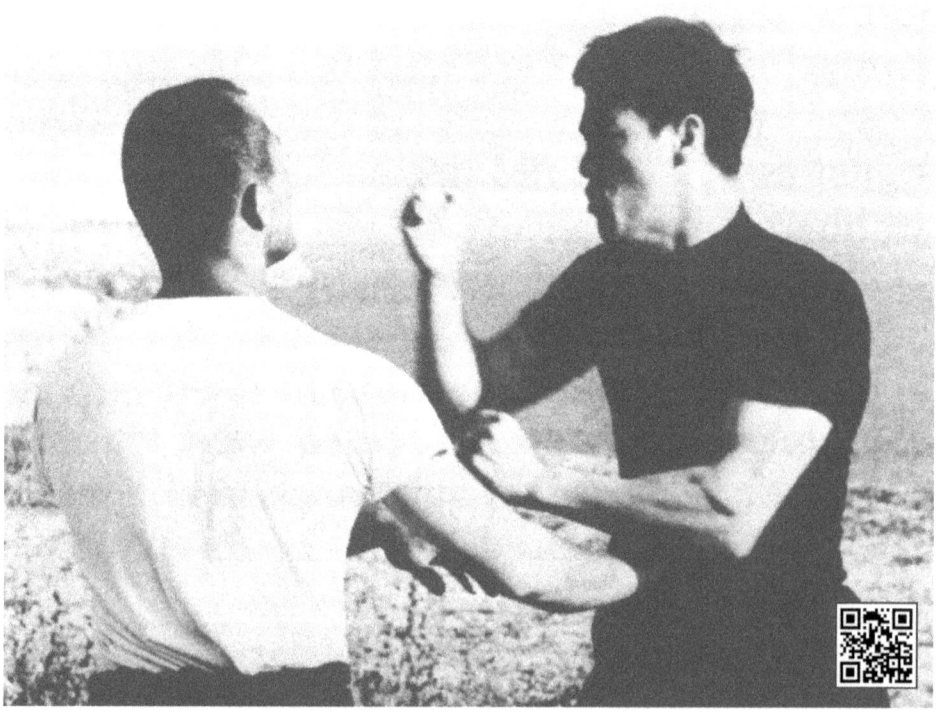

KUNG-FU MONTHLY

THE ARCHIVE SERIES
THE UNBEATABLE BRUCE LEE

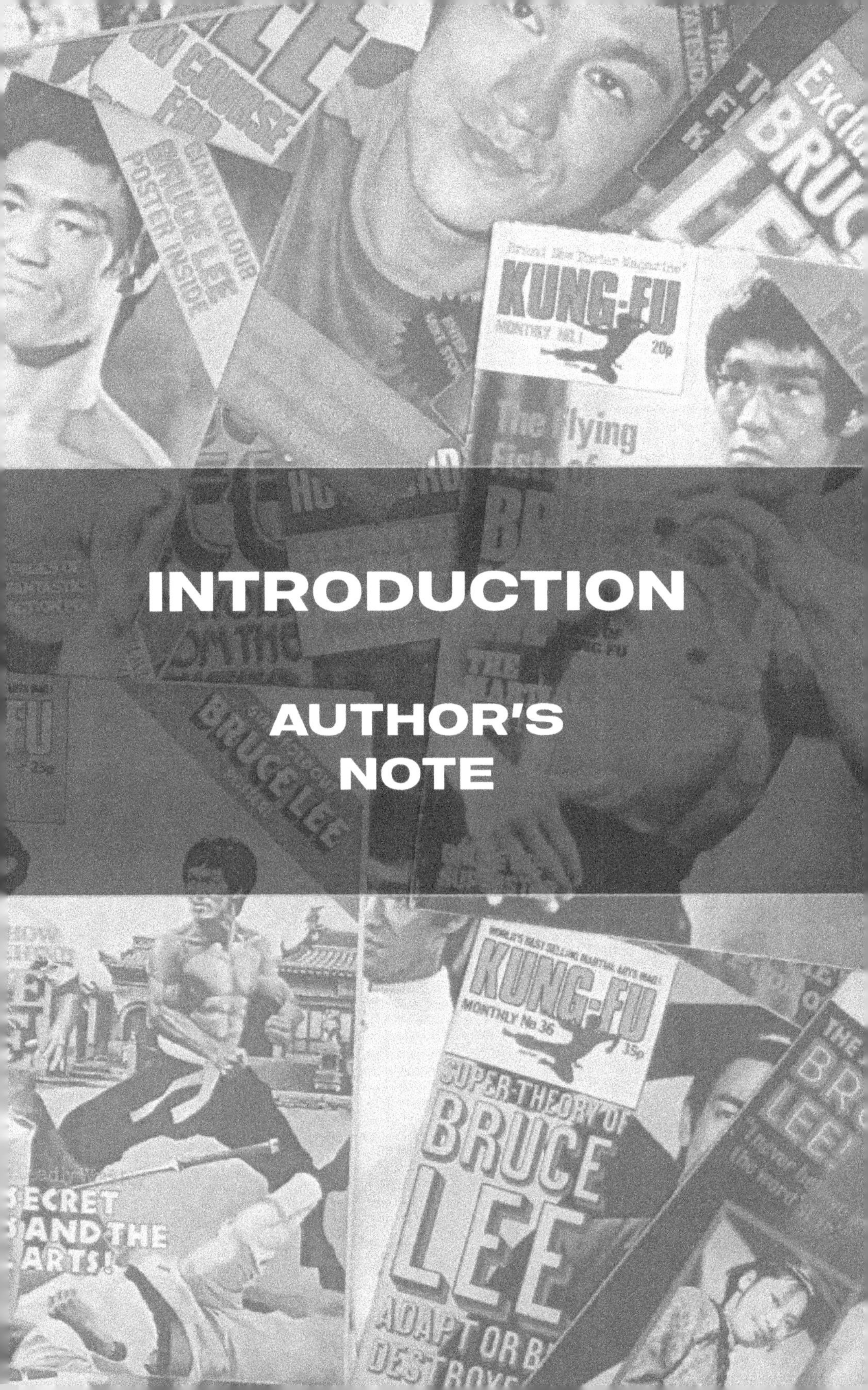

INTRODUCTION

AUTHOR'S NOTE

Throughout this book, the term Kung Fu has been used extensively. To avoid misunderstanding, some explanation is necessary.

Kung Fu or Gung Fu (Kung Fu Wu Shu to give it its full title) literally means 'work master,' or 'technique.' Any master of the martial arts can thus be described as the 'possessor' of Kung Fu, for it is not possible to translate the Chinese ideogram precisely in Western terms.

Kung Fu has been used throughout this book to denote the Chinese Martial Art for the sake of convenience and familiarity.

Ch'uan Fa (Ken Fat in Cantonese) is the Mandarin term for Chinese Boxing, or, literally, 'Way of the Fist.' 'Boxing' in this context should not be taken to mean only those techniques involving the use of the fists, but encompasses strikes and blocks using all parts of the body including the feet, as in Thai boxing or Savate.

> *"If the sword is true, the heart is true.*
> *And if the heart is true, the sword is true."*
>
> **ANCIENT CHINESE PROVERB**

What is there to say that is new about Bruce Lee?

A man, largely due to whom the term 'Kung Fu' has become virtually a household word in the West in the last eight years.

Ever since his untimely death, the Oriental martial arts have continued to grow at such a rate that they would seem destined to become a thoroughly integrated part of Western culture, adapted by each occidental to suit his own particular and individual needs.

Many stories are told of the legendary ancient masters of Kung Fu, but the majority of these hair-raising exploits can be dismissed as spurious. However, the authenticity of the abilities of the contemporary masters can be confirmed by the simple expedient of training under them, or by pictorial proof; either photographic or cinematic.

Nonetheless, there is a vast difference between a static block of wood, a pile of bricks or tiles, and a belligerent, moving, and lethal opponent who will not respond to reason, but is determined to teach one 'the error of one's ways.'

Thus we can so readily accept the mastery of Bruce Lee, by seeing his unique fighting ability epitomised on film, and subsequently by reading his words, and studying the genius captured by the photographs contained in this volume.

At an estimate, there are over 240 styles of martial arts being taught today, 200 or so of which emanate from China, and very few of which are ever taught to non-Chinese. It was for this reason that the Japanese martial arts of Judo and Karate had, until recently, taken most of the limelight in the West.

The legacy which Bruce Lee has left us then, is invaluable. Lee did much to strip away the secrecy surrounding Kung Fu and the ancestors of Japanese Bushido. a secrecy which for countless years had bordered on fetishism and as a result of which Kung Fu had remained shrouded and in the background, many styles and forms having been irrevocably lost in the process.

"I am no styles, but I am all styles," said Lee. His belief was in the free, creative martial artist who could take the best from all the classical forms, while being bound by none of them. It is not the intention to try and define Lee and. his art, for to do so would be apocryphal. Bruce Lee himself despised 'labels,' and considered the term Jeet Kune Do itself 'just a name.'

In that spirit, we present the pictures and text in this book. It is not exclusively a biography, a history, or a martial arts manual, but rather an attempt to understand the Little Dragon, a man whose entire life was an enigma.

We have tried to clarify the technique, and even to scratch a little below the surface of the technique in an effort to obtain enlightenment. Indeed, Lee himself could best have summed it up as he wrote in the introduction to his own Tao of Jeet Kune Do: "Take what is useful, and develop from there..."

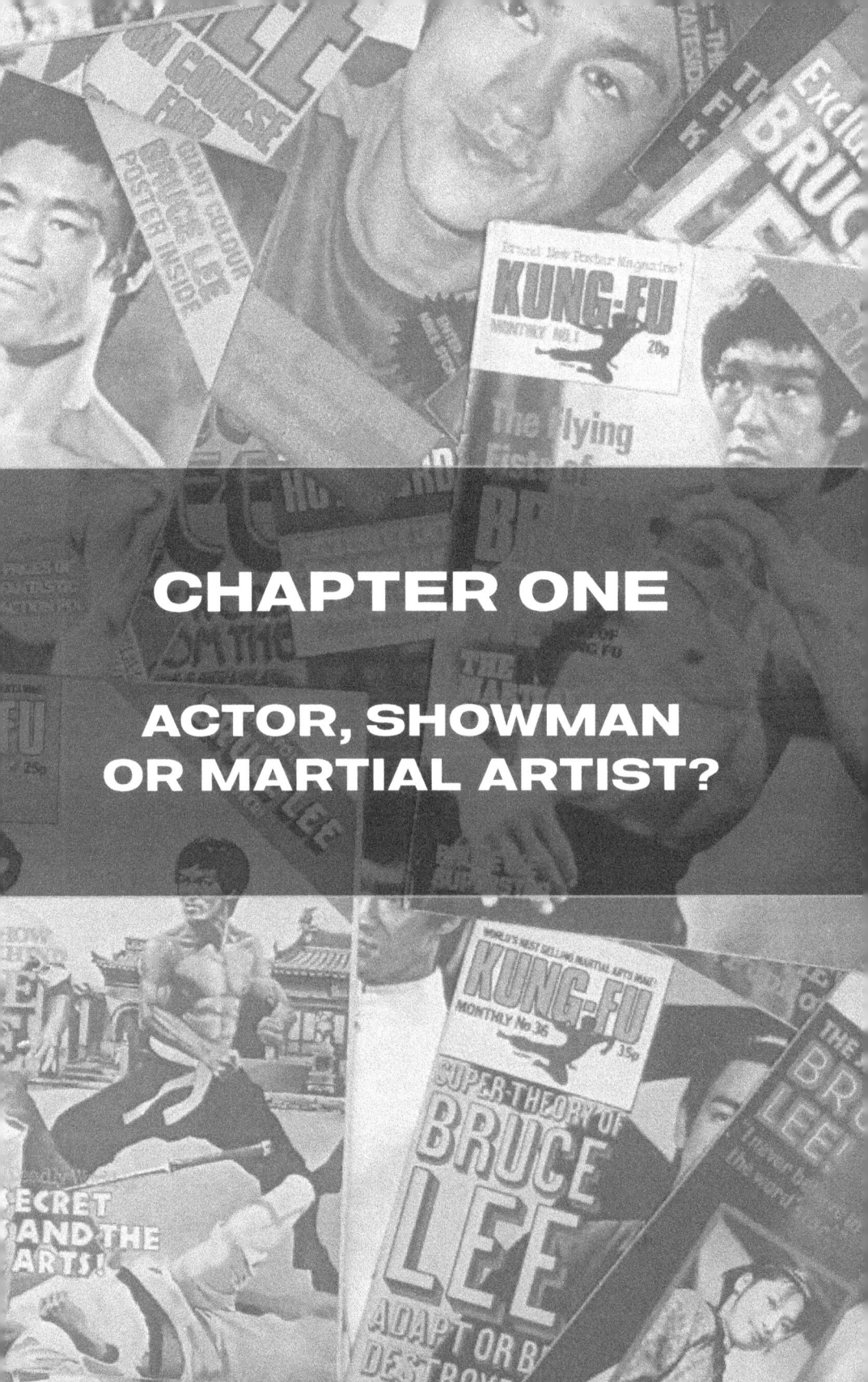

CHAPTER ONE

ACTOR, SHOWMAN OR MARTIAL ARTIST?

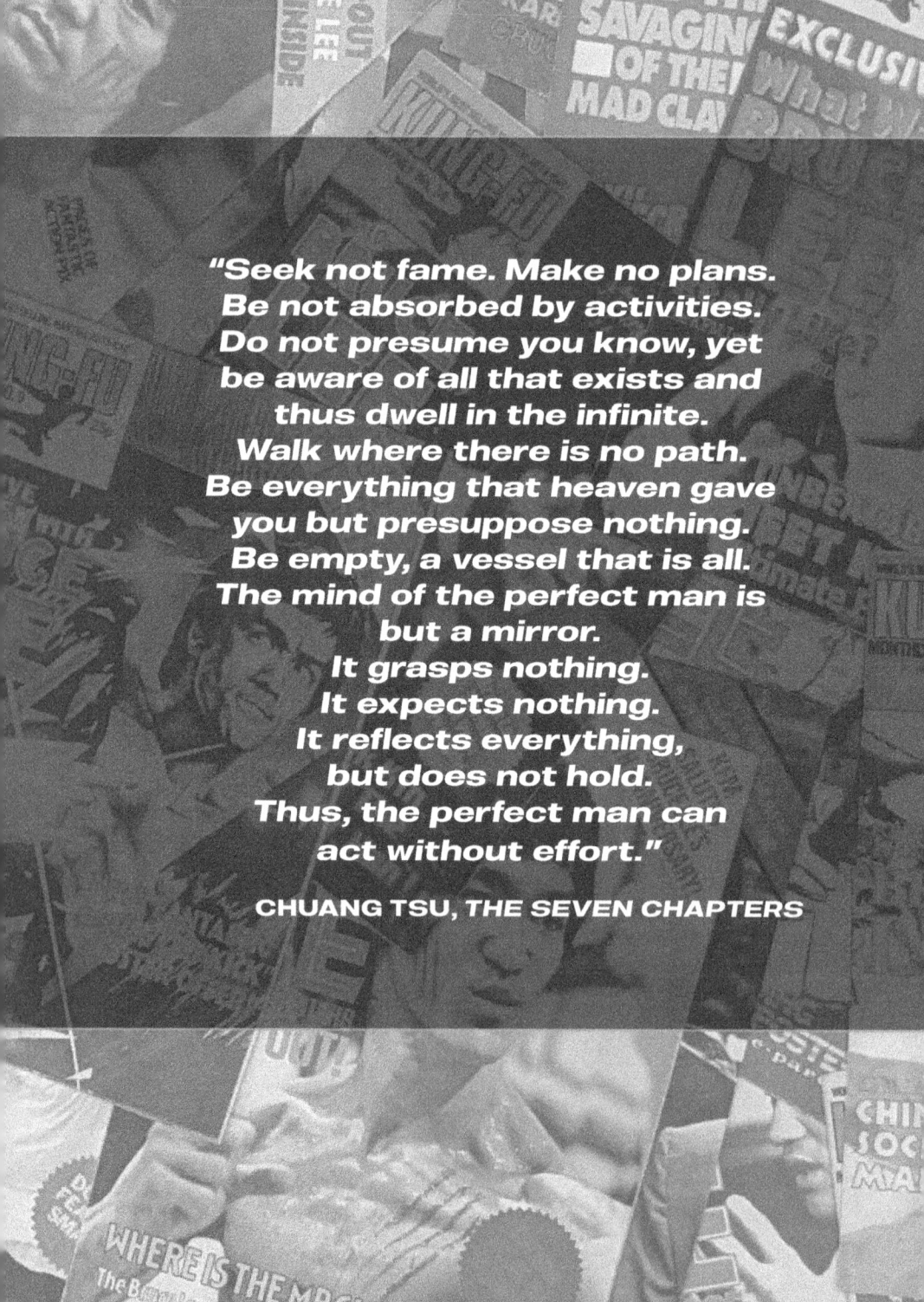

"Seek not fame. Make no plans.
Be not absorbed by activities.
Do not presume you know, yet
be aware of all that exists and
thus dwell in the infinite.
Walk where there is no path.
Be everything that heaven gave
you but presuppose nothing.
Be empty, a vessel that is all.
The mind of the perfect man is
but a mirror.
It grasps nothing.
It expects nothing.
It reflects everything,
but does not hold.
Thus, the perfect man can
act without effort."

CHUANG TSU, *THE SEVEN CHAPTERS*

Bruce Lee: Actor, Showman, or Martial Artist? The Scene: The Long Beach International Karate Championships. The Place: Long Beach, California. The Date: 1964.

In the centre of the vast auditorium, surrounded on all sides by a capacity audience of several thousands, all unbelieving, a short, well built, good looking Chinese, weighing perhaps 140 pounds, extends an invitation to the row of Karate Black Belts seated at the edge of the arena. It is not issued so much as an invitation, but a challenge.

Sceptically, a large burly Caucasian Karateka steps forward, self-consciously adjusting the black belt at his waist. He has watched this small Chinese break boards and smash bricks with a certain begrudging admiration. However, such crowd pleasing stunts were commonplace at a tournament such as this, designed as it was for Karate men to flex their muscles in public as much as for a venue where Karate men could meet, exchange ideas, and test themselves against one another.

He still cannot shake off the feeling that this new 'Kung Fu' is in no small way inferior to his own proper style of Martial Art - Karate.

He watches with surprise bordering on disbelief as the Chinese, who stands some inches shorter than himself and slighter of build, bids him to take a stance, well balanced and then walks round to position a chair three feet behind him.

Disbelief turns rapidly to incredulity, as he listens to the Chinese dictate to the crowd how he would place his fist vertically, one inch from the Black Belt's chest, and by delivering a punch from that distance, without any drawing back of his fist or movement of the feet, how he would throw the man backwards into the chair.

Calmly, the Chinese turns towards him, enquiring if he is ready, and places his fist one inch from the Karate man's chest. Although expecting no more than a heavy push, the Black Belt nevertheless tenses himself, wondering derisively what the trick is.

He is therefore totally unprepared for what is about to occur. The Chinese hardly seems to move, but his entire body is suddenly charged like the uncoiling of a huge and powerful spring. The Black Belt's one brief impression is that of a huge cat moving without visible effort, before the slightly bent arm straightens like a piston and drive the fist across the inch wide gap in a strike that is instantaneous, and frightening in its power.

The Karate man is hurled backwards into the chair. The force of the blow still carrying him, and the seat, skidding noisily across the wooden floor. Before he has realised what is happening, he has come to rest on his back, the chair tipped up, a full nine feet from the small man who now smiles benignly at him. The Chinese walks over to him, and extends a friendly hand to help him to his feet. The crowd applauds. He has just witnessed the famed One Inch Punch, performed by the one man who has ever mastered it - Bruce Lee.

How was it that Bruce Lee was able to generate such incredible power, performing seemingly impossible feats, throwing men much heavier than he, that distance with a punch that travelled a mere inch? Admittedly, these particular incidents represented very much a measure of grandstanding by Lee, a crowd pleaser designed more to promote his two newly conceived Jeet Kune Do Schools than to demonstrate the inherent qualities of Kung Fu as a philosophy and combat method. However, despite the obviously beneficial effect these demonstrations might have on his undisputed ego, Lee was passionately anxious that the American public should come to acknowledge that Kung Fu was something other than an item on the menu at a Chinese restaurant, and that, far from being merely derived from Karate, rather it was Founding Father of the Japanese Martial Art. We shall

see how in the following chapter.

Also, these demonstrations were a discipline for Lee, the breaking of bricks, tiles and boards, the pure discipline of one's powers of concentration, and of oneness with the blow.

"You must ask yourself, 'How can you honestly express yourself at that moment?' When you punch you must really want to punch - to really be in with it and express yourself. It doesn't matter how you are built, how you are made, you must go in there and be that punch."

The more traditional view is that at the instant of the strike, the entire process becomes a discipline which instantaneously unites the spirit with the total universe.

"With a single blow I smash the mirror of thirty seven years of discipline. And the great way becomes clear." Thus spoke Hojo Tokiyori, a famous thirteenth century general, who was instrumental in the speed of Zen Buddhism, and of whom Lee surely would have approved, for he showed that we are able to crash the mirror of long discipline and find enlightenment.

How the master actually physically executed these sort of techniques will be discussed in a later chapter, but that notwithstanding, much was due to his phenomenal speed. Upon watching the sequence in Enter the Dragon, where Bruce Lee fights Oharra, the henchman of the villain Han and humiliates him by striking him down several times before O'Hara can even begin to counter, a comment was made to this author by a devotee of the Martial Arts who was also a medical graduate. More in the nature of a complaint, he observed that it simply was not possible for a human being to move that quickly!

Lee's speed was notorious at various Karate tournaments where he used to demonstrate. Even some champions were apprehensive about facing him when asked to volunteer, for they knew of his prowess with fist and foot. At one tournament, while demonstrating his speed punching against a black belt volunteer, even after indicating to the victim where the punch would be directed, the black belt was unable to block the punch after eight attempts.

Lee's success lay not only with his quick hands but also with his flawless, non-telegraphic movement. The underlying concept of this is to initiate the punch or thrust without any forewarning, or "body language." That is to say, without any slight motion of feet or body.

Observe most fighters as they throw a punch. Those other than a true master will 'telegraph' the movement in some way; a slight twist of the torso perhaps, or a tensing of the shoulders, and, in some extreme cases, the street fighter or inexperienced student of the Martial Arts may even draw back the punching fist prior to striking.

All of these movements, however trifling, will signal your intention to any opponent with a practiced eye, more clearly than if you had stopped to explain it to him! However, by adopting the technique of thrusting the hand before the body, it will render the blow almost impossible to blocking or parrying.

Lee also taught the value of the "poker face" when facing an adversary. Just as card players in the game of the same title endeavour to hide their intentions behind a deadpan countenance, Lee believed that any slight twitch or change of expression - even blinking, could forewarn the opponent of his attack.

To best illustrate this, let us examine again the fight sequence with Oharra (played by

Bruce Lee, as well as for his unarmed combat, was notorious for his expertise with many of the esoteric weapons of the martial arts. Here, he demonstrates the use of the nunchaku, a weapon by now familiar to all his fans. Demonstrating the basic forward swing with the nunchaku, Lee holds one club with his right hand and releases the other. Notice how the swing is initiated and carried through using the wrist, which is straightened only at the moment of full extension or impact. Throughout, the left hand is kept in an on guard position to ward off any possible counter attacks from an opponent.

THE UNBEATABLE BRUCE LEE

The first photograph shows the on guard position for using nunchaku, the stance that Lee considered most advantageous to adopt in a combat situation. One club is held firmly in the right behind the head, with the other end resting forwards in the left palm. From this position, a lightening forward whipping strike can be made as in photo Other photos illustrate the back-handed use of the nunchaku. As a surprise tactic, from the on guard position, the nunchaku can be seized with the left hand and released by the right to perform this technique.

THE KUNG-FU MONTHLY ARCHIVE SERIES

Bob Wall) from Enter the Dragon. As Lee faces his enemy over their crossed arms, one could be forgiven for imagining that his face was carved from stone. No flicker crosses his face to betray his intention. Before anyone even realises it, he has struck, accompanied only, at the instant of the strike, by his famed shout or kiai.

Several times Lee smites Oharra down before the latter can manage to counter the lightning blows, and even when he does manage to block one, Bruce Lee counters the counter, and strikes him to his knees again.

Although Lee's films afford us a unique opportunity to observe his remarkable technique in action, despite his passing, they present some enigmas for the Martial Arts student.

Leaving aside special effects, and other cinematic excesses, Lee's fight scenes in his four major movies are as realistic as possible within the framework of the movie's narrative. Such laughable devices as hidden trampolines are almost absent here, (although some use of trampolines and springboards etc. was clearly apparent in The Big Boss for instance, this sort of technical aid virtually disappeared as Lee gained more and more control over his pictures), and the action is stripped down to its bare essentials; stark, realistic, and often bloody.

Lee is often credited with refusing to compromise on the fight scenes within his pictures by adding unnecessary frills to pad out the action. He would strip the number of blows to what he believed was a realistic minimum. If he believed that a certain blow would have rendered a man unconscious or dead, he would not have the man getting up for more, just to augment the duration of action. It was better, he believed to shoot the sequence at a faster speed and subsequently screen it in

THE UNBEATABLE BRUCE LEE

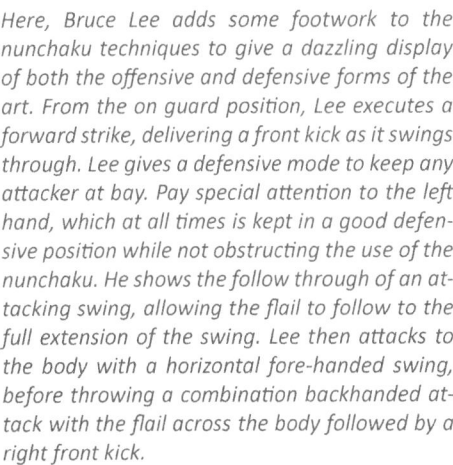
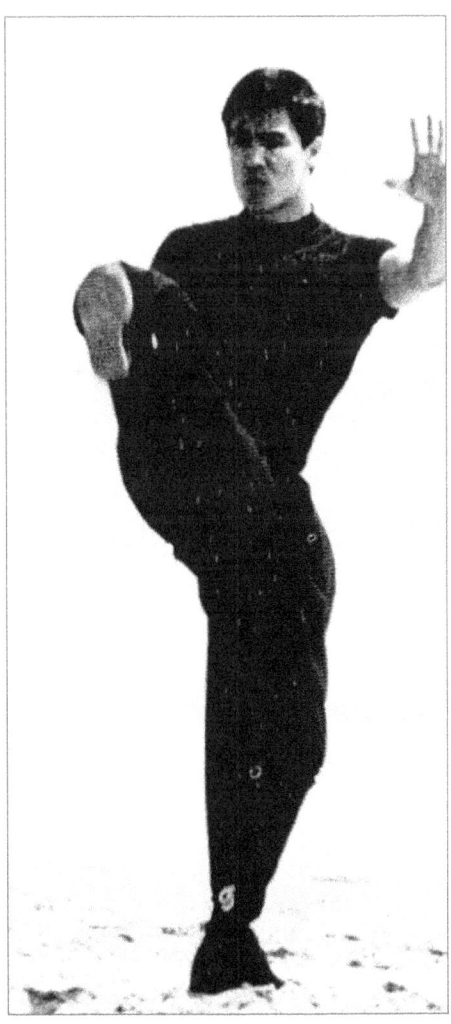

Here, Bruce Lee adds some footwork to the nunchaku techniques to give a dazzling display of both the offensive and defensive forms of the art. From the on guard position, Lee executes a forward strike, delivering a front kick as it swings through. Lee gives a defensive mode to keep any attacker at bay. Pay special attention to the left hand, which at all times is kept in a good defensive position while not obstructing the use of the nunchaku. He shows the follow through of an attacking swing, allowing the flail to follow to the full extension of the swing. Lee then attacks to the body with a horizontal fore-handed swing, before throwing a combination backhanded attack with the flail across the body followed by a right front kick.

THE KUNG-FU MONTHLY ARCHIVE SERIES

slow motion - a practice which turned out with stunning effect in fully demonstrating the devastating power of the Little Dragon's kicks and punches. Notable examples of this are where Lee is goaded into demonstrating Kung Fu to his friends in The Way of the Dragon, and sends a helper with a backstop sailing across the yard of a Chinese restaurant with a truly ferocious kick in slow motion to Oharra.

Thus, despite some cinematic licence, Lee's screen fights could be said to be fairly realistic. However, do we reconcile this with the characters that he plays?

The dazzling martial arts expertise would seem to fit uneasily on the shoulders of the heavily revenge motivated characters in The Big Boss, Fist of Fury, and Enter the Dragon who carve their way across the films leaving a wake of carnage in order to lobotomise some form of personal grief; especially to the student of Lee who has read the *Tao of Jeet Kune Do*!

"Jeet Kune Do is not to hurt, but is one of the avenues through which life opens its secrets to us. We can see through others only when we can see through ourselves, and Jeet Kune Do is a step towards knowing oneself."

Also in the Tao of Jeet Kune Do, Lee lists as one of the six 'diseases' of the martial arts; 'The desire for victory.'

We would seem to deal then, with two different sides of the coin; Bruce Lee, Actor, and Bruce Lee, Martial Artist and Philosopher.

The two came closest together in a somewhat uneasy alliance in The Way of the Dragon, on which Lee took virtually complete control as director, writer, and star. It was on often strange film, almost subdued after the more sanguinary excesses of Fist of Fury, The Big Boss, and the later extravagant Hollywood gloss of Enter the Dragon, and can be regarded rather as an embryo, a promise of things to come had Lee continued to make films over which he exerted such rigid control. Although lacking in self discipline, most probably through lack of experience and a reaction to breaking out from the shackles placed on him by other directors, it was nevertheless an interesting fusion of many of Lee's theories and experiences.

"It's a really simple plot,' he told *Esquire* magazine during filming, of a country boy going to a place where he cannot speak the language, but he comes out on top because he honestly and sincerely expresses himself by beating the hell out of everybody who gets in his way.'

Nothing could better have encapsulated Lee's own brutal, if inspired philosophy of life. But how did this man equate the 'desire for victory,' with the instinct for survival?

Some of the answers can perhaps be found in The Way of the Dragon which contained one of Lee's greatest screen fights, which itself can be seen to hold the essence of that question. The fight is with Chuck Norris, himself a world champion Black Belt, who plays a karate ace hired by the mob to dispose of Lee. The two men finally meet in a setting fitting to such an epic confrontation; the Coliseum in Rome, where once, gladiators of old also fought to the death.

The two men face each other, recognising an opponent of fearsome ability, and begin a warm up rhythm of preparatory calisthetics before, by unspoken agreement, they meet in what is certainly the toughest and most brutal piece of martial arts ever filmed.

The fight has two phases. At first, both men conforming to rigid styles, Lee trying to beat Norris by following the traditional attack and defence patterns of the classical martial

The weapon demonstrated here is a three-sectioned staff, three sturdy poles a yard long, each joined by six inches of metal chain. The long range potential of this can be seen as Bruce demonstrates a retaliation to a spear attack. Staying out of range of the spear's full extension, he makes a forehanded horizontal counter attack to his opponent's head. The longer the weapon, the more the force is magnified at the tip of the pole, so such attacks are quite devastating. Lee shows the close range capabilities of this versatile weapon. Holding one of the end poles of the nunchaku in each hand, he parries the forward spear thrust with his left, and, sinking to one knee, attacks the opponent's leading leg with his right.

arts. As a result, Lee finds he has tied himself up in his own 'classical mess,' and as a result is receiving quite a hammering.

Abruptly, inspiration strikes, and Lee changes his approach, gliding into a more fluid and flexible style, epitomising his own method of Jeet Kune Do. Norris finds that his rigid style and adherence to form cannot cope with the sudden change of pace and style. His 'rhythm' is interrupted. He has been 'psyched,' and finds his technique inadequate to counter the lightening punches and kicks with which Lee gradually pounds him to a standstill.

Suddenly, one of Lee's side kicks finds its mark on Norris' leg, and bones crunch with the sickening impact. Lee suddenly stops. With one of his favourite and most effective low line kicks, he has disabled his opponent, and now he stops and looks his opponent in the eye, shaking his head and refusing to go on.

But Norris, a professional who lives only for his art and his pride, refuses, and makes one final desperate lunging attack. Catching him in a head-lock, Lee snaps his neck.

With almost a sadness, instead of striding from the arena to face fresh battles, he pays his opponent homage by stooping to cover the prostrate body with his jacket.

By refusing to continue after disabling Norris, Lee was showing that he was not fighting by choice, and that the desire for victory here was not his driving motivation, rather the will to survive. "Give up!" he was saying to Norris. "The fight is over - there is nothing to prove!"

He has beaten his opponent, but has no wish to kill him. However, when Norris refuses to quit, Lee, however regretfully, nevertheless kills him. Survival is everything here, and Lee allows nothing to obstruct him from this end.

In all of Lee's films, attempts were made to inject some measure of Chinese philosophy of life and the martial arts, albeit clumsily at first. The example which first springs to mind is the "finger pointing at the moon" speech in Enter the Dragon. However adeptly these are handled though, however much they might appeal to the logic, they somehow fail to strike a chord in the heart, and inevitably emerge rather as 'Fortune cookie' Zen.

Despite Lee's natural charm and humour, which in spite of a somewhat unpolished acting technique still managed to shine through in a unique screen presence. Lee was at his best in his martial arts sequences, where he was most able to express himself to the full.

The martial combat sequences were not 'acting' for Lee though, for despite the fact that getting them onto celluloid represented no mean feat of staging and engineering, they were a simple representation of Lee doing what naturally came best to him.

It can therefore be said, without fear of contradiction, that the Coliseum fight in Way of the Dragon embodies all that is best in the Little Dragon's movies, the excitement, spectacular action, the philosophies it represents, and of course, the incomparable technique.

Linda Lee writes that her husband considered himself a martial artist first and an actor second, and no-one could disagree with that. Whatever the future might have held with regard to his acting career, we shall of course, never know.

Showman? Perhaps; but only in pursuit of his quest to bring his Martial Art to the attention of a wide public so that Jeet Kune Do might outlive even it's creator and continue to live on amongst his students, friends, and countless fans.

But above all, Bruce Lee was indeed a martial artist per excellence, an undisputed master, at whose feats we can only marvel, and whose art we can only admire.

Somewhat uncharacteristically, Bruce Lee demonstrates various positions of attack using the spear. Although it is not generally known to many of his fans, Lee was more than adept with most non-explosive hand weapons, including sticks, spears, bonsai etc. The first photographs show the on guard position in the cat stance, similar to that of the nunchaku, and demonstrate another variation of this from the forward leaning stance. The final photograph shows a one-handed lunge.

In any combat situation, the on-guard stance or position is the foundation on which the techniques are built. Indeed, an experienced fighter can usually assess the calibre of his opponent from the stance that he adopts. The Jeet Kune Do on guard position is explored further in chapter 3 of this book, but here, Bruce Lee shows four other hand positions. The first image shows the basic fist position usually adopted by beginners. The clenched fist is usually encouraged in less advanced students who tend to have less powerful hands and wrists than the more practiced aficionado. The leading arm is held forward, bent at 45°, with the other hand held back in a defensive position at the chest. Images above show the traditional snake strike and dragon's claw respectively. The snake position is used for whipping and darting strikes to the soft areas of face and neck, while the dragon's claw is manifested in a more stabbing and tearing technique. The photograph below shows the enticement position, generally used by only very advanced martial artists.

The technique of simultaneous attack as a defence is one requiring perfect balance and timing, shown here with complete mastery by the Little Dragon. As his opponent attacks with a right handed punch, Lee simultaneously launches an attack with his right arm, driving under his opponent's thrust, using his arm and shoulder to deflect it - in effect, a parry and counter-attack in one. Demonstrating his phenomenal speed, he then launches a left handed dragon's claw thrust to his opponent's groin.

THE KUNG-FU MONTHLY ARCHIVE SERIES

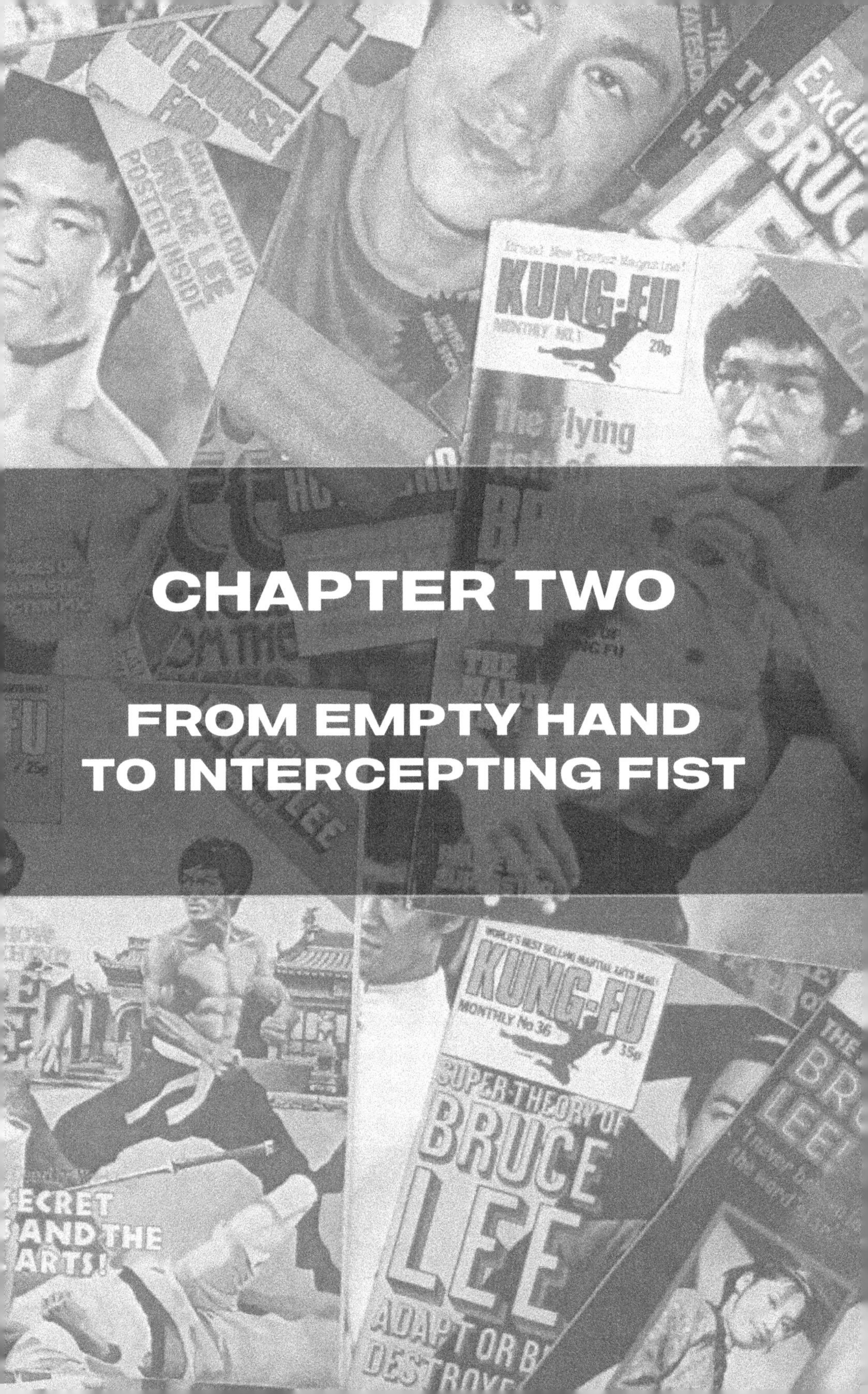

CHAPTER TWO

FROM EMPTY HAND TO INTERCEPTING FIST

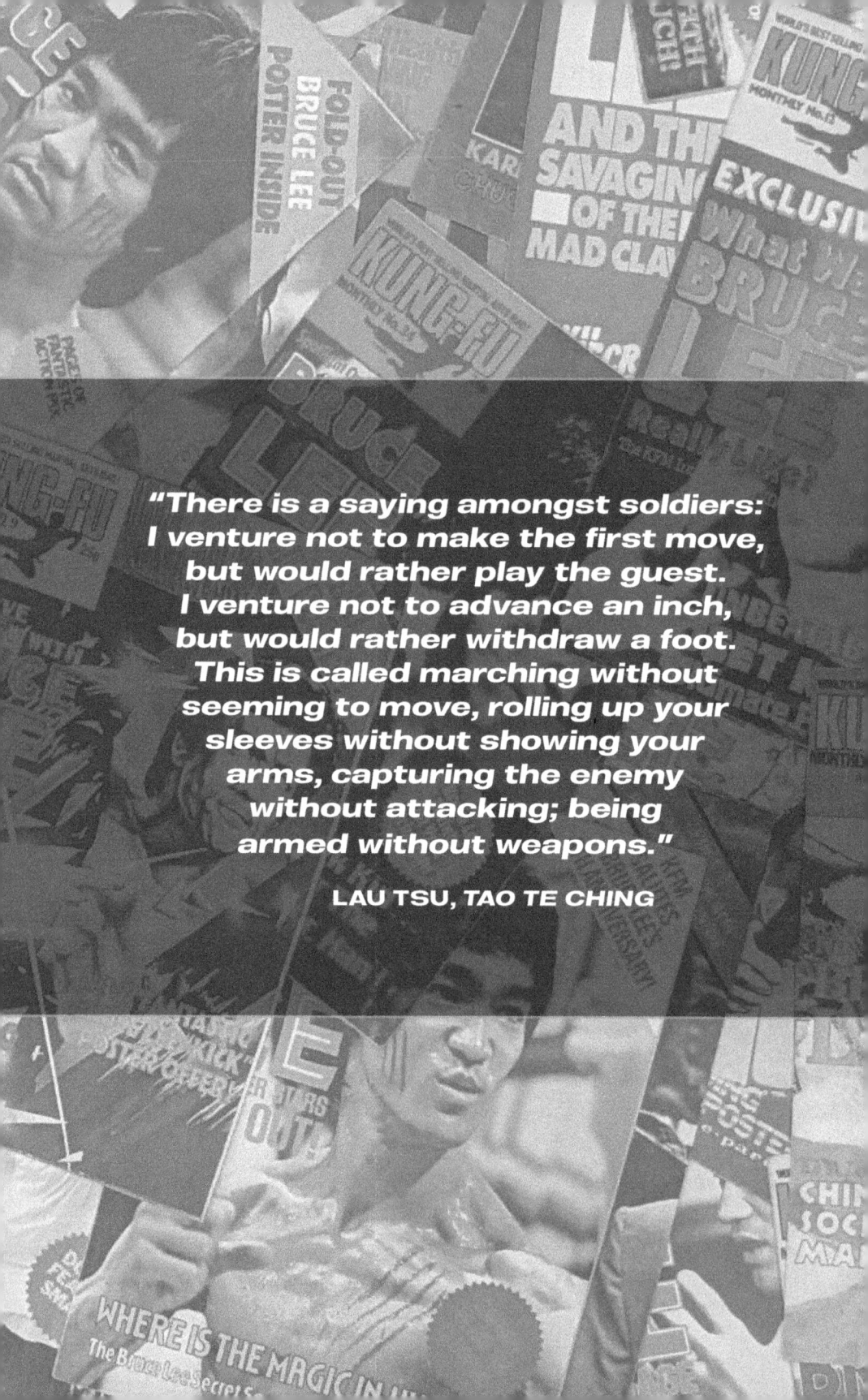

"There is a saying amongst soldiers: I venture not to make the first move, but would rather play the guest. I venture not to advance an inch, but would rather withdraw a foot. This is called marching without seeming to move, rolling up your sleeves without showing your arms, capturing the enemy without attacking; being armed without weapons."

LAU TSU, *TAO TE CHING*

In the widest sense, Kung Fu, like all other means of bare-handed fighting, must have originated with man himself, for, since the earliest times, he has constantly been at battle with either the beasts around him, or with his fellow man. Kung Fu as a rationalised technique however did not appear until men began to live together in communities.

Who is to say therefore, that Kung Fu owes its earliest origins to either Orient or Occident, as at this stage of civilisation, cultures all over the world were developing styles of fighting that resemble in some way the modern Martial Arts. Insofar as the basics of hand to hand fighting could be described as the common property of mankind, Kung Fu itself belongs to the world at large, and although in its ways and forms today it is definitely Oriental, there is nothing to forbid its mastery by peoples everywhere.

The oldest known records concerning techniques or unarmed combat are hieiroglyphic scrolls from Egyptian tombs, which date back to 4000 B.C.

In these, description are to be found of military training fights similar to modern boxing, even advocating the use of a leather glove which extended to the elbow. 1000 years later, boxing and wrestling were being practiced in the Sumerian Kingdom of Mesopotamia, and murals from the Beri-Hassan tomb in Egypt show that in about 2300 B.C., a more refined form of boxing had developed, one which was later to cross the Mediterranean to Greece.

By about 300 years later, both boxing and wrestling had become popular with the Minoan civilisation an ancient Crete which built a temple to the goddess Hera where they held games of both military and religious events.

In 2000 B.C. came invasion by the Ionians, closely followed to Greece by the Agaeans, in 1800 B.C., both of whom were to follow the traditions of their predecessors in holding games to the god Zeus. It was not until 1580 B.C. however, that both the games to Zeus and those to Hera were combined to form the first Olympian meet.

Due to the Dorian invasions of the twelfth century B.C., the games were not resumed until 776 B.C., and wrestling was to make its appearance as an official event in the eighteenth games in 700 B.C.

Boxing however did not reappear until twelve years later when it was included in the twenty third games of 688 B.C.

Theagenes, the most noted boxer of the fifth century B.C. is reputed to have conquered 2,102 adversaries by knockouts, and to have killed 1,800. Indeed, the combat was violent, and many of the combatants were wounded or killed.

Of Milo, the greatest wrestler of the period, it was written that he trained by lifting a calf every day, continuing to do so until it became a fully grown cow. According to Quintillius, another incredible feat performed by this giant was to carry a cow around the Olympian arena before killing it with a single blow and eating it by himself. His legendary appetite lead him to consume eighteen pounds of meat and bread, and vast amounts of wine every day!

In the thirty-third games (648 B.C.), all rules were removed when the pancratium came into conception; a primitive form of Kung Fu, sometimes cited as the predecessor of modern wrestling. It was a particularly vicious sport which allowed the use of all parts of the body. The only fouls were biting and gouging, and the contest continued until one person gave up. Of all the ancient combative arts, the pancratium best encapsulated Lee's own theory that the object of combat was to win at any cost.

THE UNBEATABLE BRUCE LEE

Here, the attacker has moved forward with a right-handed attack. Lee defends with his left hand, hooking and trapping his opponent's wrist, pulling it down and forwards to bring the man off balance and into position for a counter attack - in this case, a backhanded knife hand blow or jab. Other photographs show a possible spear hand thrust to the eyes or throat. Lee disdains close quarters defence, and attacks from long range with a roundhouse kick, very effective to the head and neck. The final photograph shows the front stamp kick, either up under the chin (if performed at the necessary speed), or to the torso or groin.

Against his friend and student Dan Inosanto, himself a black belt, Bruce Lee shows a sequence of stunning attacks and defence. He blocks his opponent's right punch, and traps the arm at the wrist, pulling it forwards to pull his man off balance. Immediately, he attacks the elbow of the arm with a forearm smash. Without pause, and using the same arm, he delivers a backhanded inverted fist blow to his opponent's head. Now pushing his opponent's arm down and away with this same left hand, he throws a right leading punch to the face. Another variation of this is also shown. Here, the right punch has been blocked with the left hand, trapped and pulled sideways to open the opponent up for a snake strike to the face or palm heel blow up under the chin.

To what extent the germs of a seed which were sown in Ancient Greece were borne on the winds of invasion to germinate and take root in India is not fully known, for no artefacts or records exist to describe combat techniques prior to the Arian invasions of the twelfth and tenth century B.C. However, it is reasonable to conclude that the origins of Yoga were practiced by people of the indigenous Indus culture. Although not attributable to either combative or religious regimes, Yoga has nevertheless exerted a far reaching influence on all of the Oriental Martial Arts. In the fifth and sixth centuries B.C. Yoga was first codified by the Arians, in the same period that Indian combat techniques were first recorded. Combat techniques were later to be classified into forms of striking, seizing, and joint techniques in the famous Lotus Sutra, and in the fourth and third centuries B.C., these categories were to become well established as separate developments of the Martial Art.

At the time that Gautama Siddartha, (the Buddha) lived on earth, much of India was divided into sixteen secular factions, all of which were warring against each other. The most powerful of these, the Brahmins, believed that every man's duty was to become an itinerant priest and consequently, since these wanderers were often forced to defend themselves against wild animals and villagers of different religious persuasions, combat training was of paramount importance.

Gautama himself, reputed to have been a man of peace and love was nonetheless a prince, and as such received military training. Indeed, so skilful is he said to have become, that he was never to be defeated. Legend also tells us that he was able to overcome all evil spirits by dazzling them with the reflection from the nimbus which surrounded his body, more probably an indication that he used many of the lightening fast movements to develop in Chinese boxing, or Ch'uan Fa.

As the Arians had devastated the culture of the Indus during the invasions, it would suggest superior weapons and advanced combat technology, brought with them from an origin in common with that of Greek boxing and wrestling. However it was during this period that the bare handed techniques of the Indian continent were to be espoused with Yoga to attain their indigenous Indian nature.

Above all though, China was to act as the catalyst in developing and refining techniques now referred to as Kung Fu. The formalised calisthetics practised by the Chinese since about 2500 B.C. would seem to indicate that some form of combat technique was being developed in China during the years before Bodhidharma arrived there in 520 A.D. The legendary twenty eighth patriarch of Buddhism, Bodhidharma (Ta Mo) was the third son of the Indian King Sugandha, a brilliant student of Zen, and was to become the leading light of early Kung Fu.

After the death of his mentor, the priest Prajnatara, Bodhindharma resolved to travel on foot to China, where he had heard that Buddhism had been transmitted in a debased form.

After a long and arduous journey, Bodhidharma arrived at the court of the Emperor Wu in Chin Lung, the province of Liang. After a brief and unsuccessful period there, due to fundamental disagreements of doctrine, Bodhidharma was expelled, and travelled northwards to the Kingdom of Wei, eventually arriving at the Shaolin monastery on Hao-shan, a mountain on the lower reaches of the Yangtze river. Since 386 A.D., the Shaolin monastery had been famous as a spiritual and physical training ground for priests, but on Bodhidhar-

Still on California's Malibu beach, Bruce Lee demonstrates the essence of Jeet Kune Do's effectiveness as a combat method in close quarters fighting. As Inosanto throws a left leading punch, he parries with a palm heel outside block, deflecting the punch past his head, and bending the knees slightly, attacks to the solar plexus with a straight right punch. Lee then performs a block and trap to the left wrist, followed by a low line side stamp kick to the knee. Lee was a great believer in this technique, as kicking downwards at 45°, it requires only 60 lbs of pressure to dislocate the knee joint. Once disabled in this way he taught, an opponent was as good as dead. Lee's assailant throws a right punch, which Lee chops downwards with his left hand into the man's elbow, bending his arm, and throwing a right punch to the head. Alternatively, he anticipates the attack, and leaping forwards he seizes the leading arm of his partner. Forestalling the attack while simultaneously attacking himself with his fist to the head. At close range, Lee ties up his opponent with his left arm, while attacking to the chin with short sharp fist and inverted knuckle strikes. At longer range, he smashes aside his opponent's guard and attacks with side or roundhouse kicks.

ma's arrival, he found most of the monks in poor physical condition. To improve their skill in combat, he was to fuse his own knowledge of Yoga breath discipline with indigenous Chinese Ch'uan Fa. Bodhidharma had also brought with him two texts from India, the I-chin-ching and the Hsien-siu-ching, the former in particular concerned with practical methods of the military arts.

From these, he was to introduce the set of physical drills named 'Shi Pa Lo Han Sho' eighteen hands of the Lo Han, the basis of what is now known as Shaolin boxing.

Ch'uan Fa as practiced at the Shaolin monastery was originally kept a close secret, and was taught only to those of the Buddhist priesthood, and who had entered the monastery.

THE UNBEATABLE BRUCE LEE

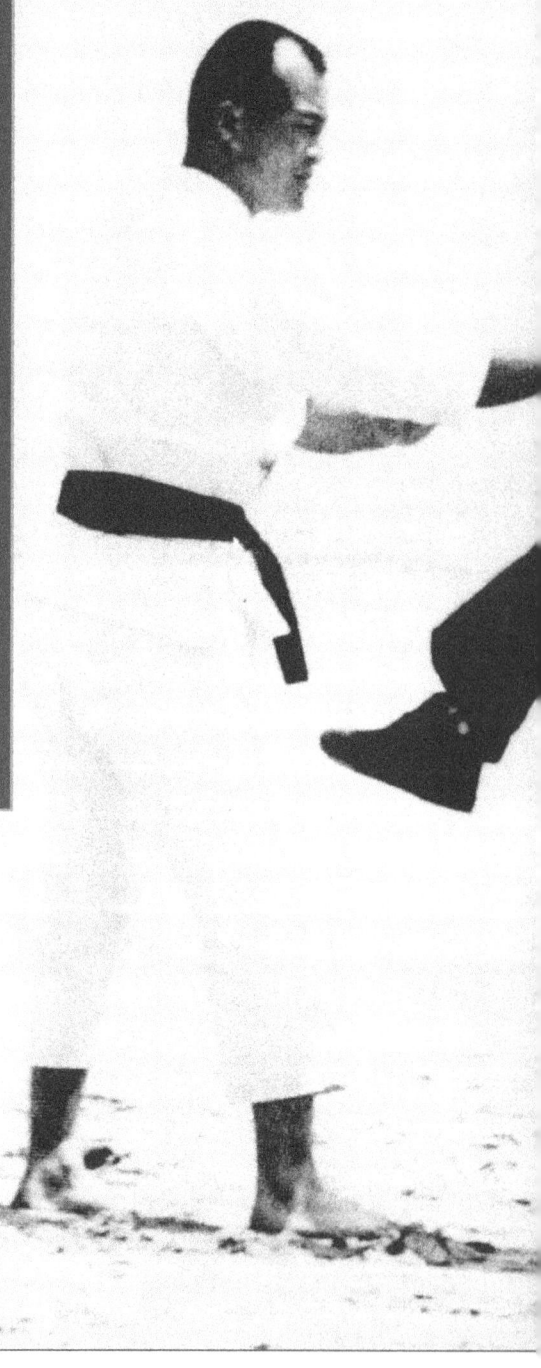

Dan Inosanto throws another right handed attack against Lee. He uses a palm heel parry to his opponent's fist and attacks with a front kick to the groin. Using a knife hand block to the inside of Inosanto's wrist in photograph, he uses his hand to trap the attacking arm, and counter attacks to the solar plexus in this shot. In another variation, Lee blocks the arm downwards and uses a snake strike to the eyes, or alternatively a tiger claw blow to the face. He traps the right arm with his own right hand, and turning his body outside the line of attack, applies pressure to the elbow joint with his left hand, forcing his opponent down. Lee deflects the attack with his upper arm, and stepping outside his opponent's arm can attack to the unprotected ribcage with an elbow strike. Dan Inosanto blocks Lee's roundhouse kick to the head with a high line inside block, while Bruce deflects a kick to the groin with a low line palm heel block. Note his left hand always held in the defensive position to cover the head and body.

At this stage, the eighteen point system was probably not intended for aggressive purposes, but later government persecutions and repeated burnings of the temple destroyed the Shaolin and dispersed the monks. During these times, weapons were banned, and the monks trained at the Shaolin felt it their duty to each Ch'uan Fa to the oppressed masses as a protection against both bandits and corrupt government officials. Thus, Ch'uan Fa, minus its original Zen elements, began a gradual spread among the people in various parts of China. After the I-Ching reached the general public, it lost its connection with Bodhidharma's concept of the unity of body and soul, and began to develop as a separate combat technique.

The techniques were transmitted either in fragments, or one by one, and the Shaolin temple itself has little connection with the later history of Chinese boxing. After the burning of the temple by the emperor Wu Ti (A.D. 574) and its subsequent rebuilding during the Siu Dynasty (589-618) there is no evidence of Ch'uan Fa, and it seems to have disappeared entirely from the site of its introduction into China to survive amongst the people themselves.

By the time of the T'ang (seventh to tenth centuries) skill in unarmed fighting had become a requirement of military service, and from the latter part of the Sung (947-1279) until the Ch'ing Dynasty (1662-1912) Ch'uan Fa enjoyed what was to be called its golden age. Myriad styles and forms were to flourish prior to the banning of Ch'uan Fa in China by the Manchu government in 1900, largely as a result of the infamous and abortive Boxer rebellion of 1896.

According to the most widely accepted legend, it was during the sixteenth and seventeenth centuries that Wing Chun Kung Fu was to originate, although as with the birth of other styles, much of the Chinese Martial Arts' history is shrouded in secrecy.

The founding matriarch of Wing Chun (Beautiful Springtime) was Yim Wing Chun, a woman who studied the Martial Arts under a Shaolin nun Ng Miu. Like Bruce Lee, who was to follow her four centuries later, she became disillusioned with the traditional style, coming to believe more and more than Ch'uan Fa was in danger of becoming bogged down by elaborate stances and a disproportionate emphasis on brute strength.

Leaving her Shaolin tutor, Madame Yim set out to develop an entirely new style of combat, taking much of what she had already learned but combining it with a radical new set of concepts to form a much more fluid and flexible form of combat, eminently suitable for fighting at close quarters.

From the thirty eight forms or 'katas' of the Shaolin system. Madame Yim Wing Chun distilled just three. Forms, she believed, led to a too rigid style, unable to adapt to the requirements of actual combat. What she hoped to develop was a softer system, owing much to the contribution of Chang Sarfeng of the Sung period (tenth to thirteenth centuries). Chang retired to the mountains to perfect his own version of the fighting technique he had learned while studying at the Shaolin, adding a certain gentleness to the hard system, and placing more of an emphasis on self defence. His basic principle involves soft, elegant action in blocking techniques, and sudden, sharp, powerful blows when the moment is right, supposedly evolved from watching a crane attacked by a snake. While forced to retreat, the crane made soft, rounded movements with its wings, but, as soon as an opportunity afforded itself, it darted at its enemy with a powerful and speedy beak.

The style which Madame Yim was to hand down through seven generations uses the

opponent's strength rather than trying to defeat it by meeting it head on. There is a name for this technique; rysin, or flowing water, which derives from the fact that, instead of attempting to stop your opponent's attack, you let it flow by, leaving you untouched. Joining your strength to your adversary's attack, and allowing it to go in its own direction, you can increase the destructive power of your own strike.

By flowing with the opponent, unhampered by unnecessary preconceptions, the Wing Chun fighter is capable of defending himself even when fighting blindfolded. The basis of Wing Chun is its simplicity. Stripped of burdening movements, its essence can be learned effectively in a shorter time than other styles which rely heavily on traditional stances and set forms.

While other styles of the period were very heavily based on the rationalisations of Chiao Yuan, a famous Shaolin priest of the thirteenth century -the five animals (the Dragon, the Tiger, the Leopard, the Snake, and the Crane), which were later to be integrated into 170 movements based on the eighteen hands of Lo Han by Pai Yu-Feng and Chueh Yuan, a Shaolin monk. Wing Chun Kung Fu went in much the opposite direction.

Although regarded by some as prostituting the original concepts of Bodhidharma in the eternal search for mammon, Ip Man, sixth generation master of Wing Chun realised that an easily adaptable system of close defence and swift attack was badly needed. In many ways, Ip Man was the founding father of modern Wing Chun, a tough and wiry immigrant from Kwantung province who had spent most of his life practicing, perfecting, and finally, refining the art. It was Ip Man who had brought Wing Chun out from behind the Bamboo Curtain, along with many other exponents of Ch'uan Fa who had fled from the communist regime to settle in Hong Kong.

And thus it was that one day in 1953, a thirteen year old youth walked into Ip Man's classes to enrol for a course in the lethal art of Chinese Kung Fu. An uncontrollable teenager, already leader of a street gang, and well on the way to carving out a career for himself on the streets and in the back alleys of Hong Kong, Lee was not interested in (even if he was aware of) a monk called Bodhidharma, even less in the unification of body and soul. What he needed was a better way of beating people up.

'One day I wondered what would happen if I got into a fight without a gang behind me,' he told Black Belt magazine in -a 1967 interview, 'So I decided to learn how to protect myself and I began to study Kung Fu.'

Martial Arts training is based on strict discipline, and this in itself limits the number of students who will ever climb to the heady heights of real proficiency. The rigorous training of most accredited schools soon alienates the majority of beginners the dabbler, the indolent, the undisciplined, and those with no liking for competition or physical training. Young thugs who join merely as a means towards a violent end are usually weeded out by the basic training itself, realising it will take many years of dedicated and concerted training to even glimpse the true possibilities.

Only those who see something more, something within themselves will survive this long course. And so it was with Bruce Lee.

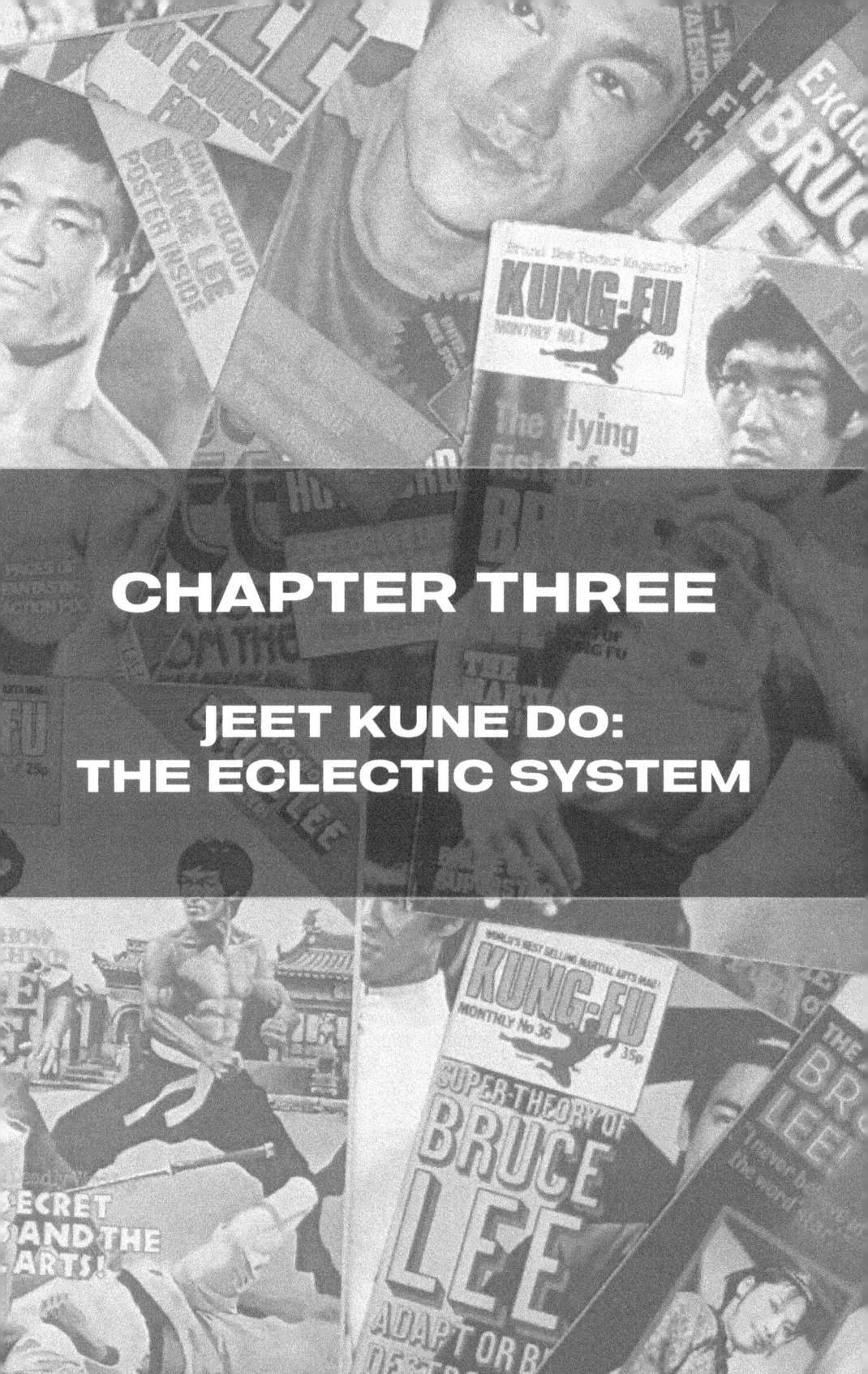

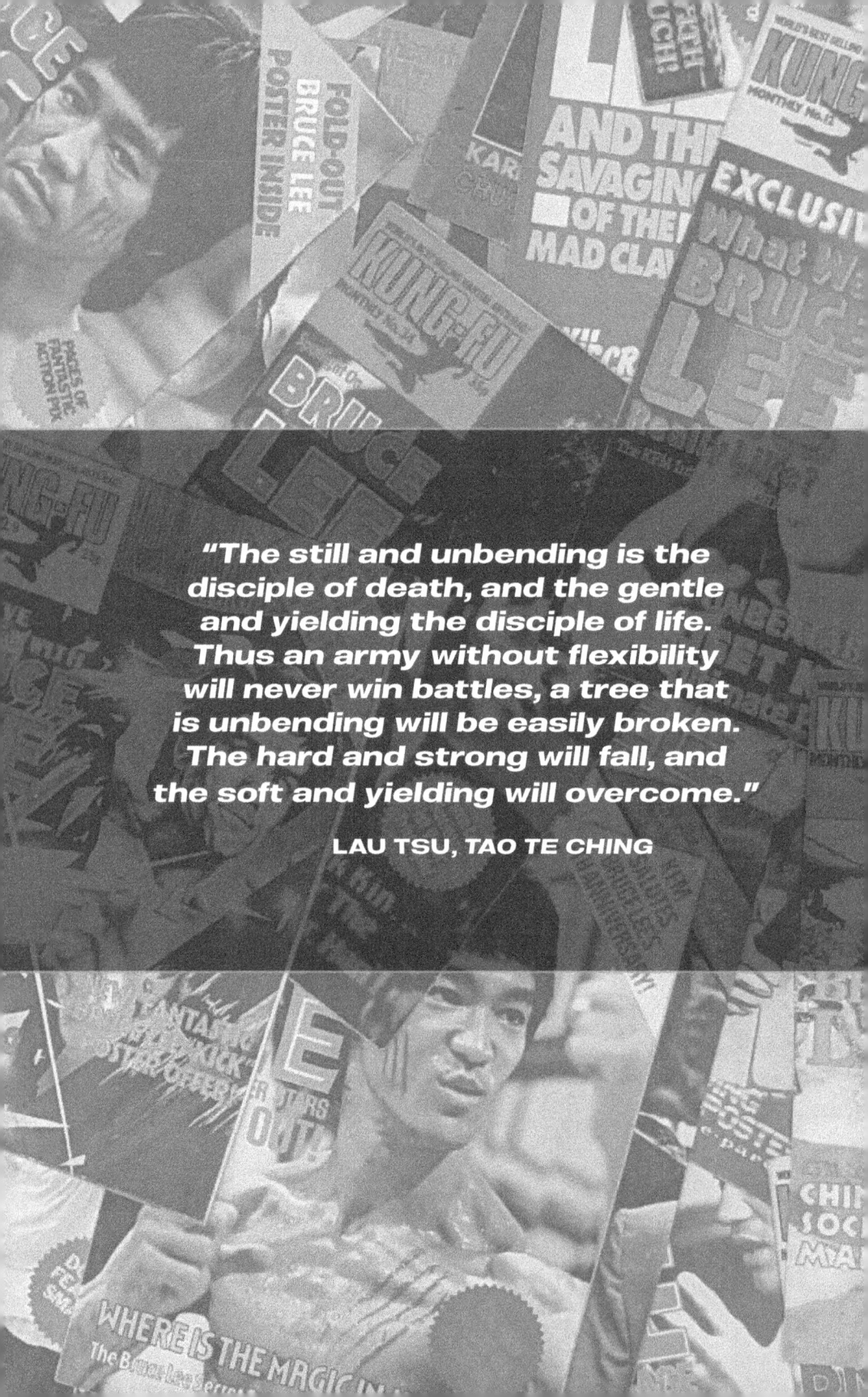

"The still and unbending is the disciple of death, and the gentle and yielding the disciple of life. Thus an army without flexibility will never win battles, a tree that is unbending will be easily broken. The hard and strong will fall, and the soft and yielding will overcome."

LAU TSU, *TAO TE CHING*

As everyone knows, the five human senses are sight, sound, smell, taste and touch. Through the sense of sight, we are able to appreciate nature, colours, paintings, and everything we can perceive through the eyes. The sense of sound enables us to hear the spoken word, music and all the other sound of the world around us. Through our sense of smell, we are aware of the aromas borne on the air. The five tastes: sweet, bitter, salty, sour and astringent give us the enjoyment of the table and the cup. Our sense of touch tells us when things are hard or soft, hot or cold, smooth or rough.

But beyond all these five, there lies yet another, a sixth sense, one which collect all the impression and information perceived by the other five, and through an intuitive application cause and effect, gives rise to the process of logical reasoning. The sixth sense could be defined as perception or intuition. It is not like the five senses - the reception of outside stimuli or phenomena - but is rather an indirect spiritual and metaphysical perception, and as such, essential to the martial arts.

The inner value of the martial arts does not involve the necessity of instruction in supernatural power, nor should there be need for conscious study, rather it should come about through a fostering of the sixth sense depending on the accumulation of direct experience through the five basic senses. The master of the martial arts who has attained this 'inner truth,' is stronger than all others, for he has no need to rely on other weapons.

The way towards mastery of the martial arts is firstly to learn the techniques and methods, then to refine the spirit. At this point, the Oriental martial arts and zen are inseparably linked. These underlying psychological principles have received much notice in the western world recently, in fact, largely due to the Kung Fu 'boom' and the subsequent search for nirvana, they probably receive more comment than they do in their home countries.

The basic psychological principles of the martial arts are stated as concentration, calmness, and confidence. The latter quality is obtained as a result of proficiency in the application of the former two. The Kung Fu exponent should strive for total awareness of his opponent's reactions, but while allowing his own thoughts to flow freely, and not considering his opponent's movements and reactions in predetermined patterns.

Was it this sixth sense, this intuition and inner calm that Bruce Lee found within himself that was to enable him to endure the rigorous course of the martial arts that was to drive him on until his training enveloped him to the point of fanaticism? It was not a process which happened overnight, but certainly Ip Man must have perceived at least a glimmer of it in the taciturn thirteen year old, for under Ip Man's intuitive guidance, Lee was eventually to refine, distil, and mature into a philosopher, master, and innovator of the martial arts.

Ip Man was inevitably possessed of this 'inner sense,' as was Lee in his later development, although it was not until much later that a philosophy major at Seattle University was to enable him to articulate this sense and to record his thoughts on the matter in the Tao of Jeet Kune Do.

"Jeet Kune Do avoids the superficial, penetrates the complex, goes to the heart of the problem, and pinpoints the Key Factors," wrote Lee in 1970. "Jeet Kune Do is the enlightenment. It is a way of life, a movement towards will power and control, though it ought to be enlightened by intuition."

Ip Man must have sensed the inner strength in Lee which singled him out from the

THE KUNG-FU MONTHLY ARCHIVE SERIES

As his opponent attempts a right-handed attack, Lee parries with his right forearm, leaving him open to attack his assailant with his left arm.

Good naturedly, he points out to Inosanto how easy it is to penetrate his defence from this technique. As Dan Inosanto tries a back-handed fist strike to penetrate Lee's defence, the Little Dragon steps forward to parry with his left palm, using the same arm to immediately deliver a knuckle-punch to his opponent's head. As a follow-up technique in this instance, Lee uses either the front stamp-kick using the ball or heel of the foot to his opponent's abdomen, or a leaping front kick. The advantage of the leaping front kick is that it can often take an opponent by surprise, causing him to raise his guard, leaving his body unprotected, and drive him back. It also has the added advantage of carrying some of

the forward body momentum into the kick, which is made at the apex of the jump. As his assailant attacks again to the head, Lee falls back into a crouch, out of effective range. Inosanto now attempts a roundhouse kick to the abdomen. Lee blocks with a low line forearm block, driving the hard outside edge of his arm into the shin in order to hurt his opponent as well as stopping the blow. Momentarily distracted by the pain, and also off balance, Inosanto is defenceless as Lee immediately retaliates with a lunging front kick to the groin.

THE UNBEATABLE BRUCE LEE

This time, Lee's attacker tries a side kick with the left foot. Before the blow can reach him, Lee parries with a low-line block with his right arm, driving into his opponent's shin with the hard outside edge of the forearm, and driving the kick to his right. Not discouraged, his attacker attempts a left spear hand thrust to the face. In this case, Bruce simply uses a lean-back dodge. Note how he keeps his rear hand high in the defensive position, keeps his knees bent to maintain good balance, and leans only the torso backwards in a fluid motion to stay out of range of the job. The technique is that of ryusui - flowing water - allowing the opponent's attack to expend itself. Lee springs his torso back, using the fluid rebounding action to lend momentum to a retaliatory spear thrust to his opponent's face.

other students, and was to try to develop it; to channel the youngster's aggressive energies back into a realisation of the true heart of Kung Fu.

Certainly, trying to instil some of the deeper meanings into the unmanageable teenager must have, at first, been an unrewarding process. After his first few lessons with Ip Man, some basic Kung Fu added to his street fighting expertise, Lee would prowl the alleys and backstreets searching for some hapless victim on whom to test what he had just learned.

For whatever reasons at this stage, Bruce Lee nevertheless threw himself wholeheartedly into his Kung Fu training. There are many stories of Lee as a youngster practicing diligently day and night, and thumping his free hand against the leg of his stool to toughen it as he was eating, but Ip Man was to persevere, and as the years passed, Kung Fu became a steadying influence on Lee. Within three years, he had become Wing Chun Kung Fu's star pupil.

The old master tried to impart to his pupil the technique of Ryusui - Flowing Water, which had been handed down from Madame Yim.

"Preserve yourself by following the natural flow of things and do not interfere," he imparted to his protege. "Remember never to assert yourself against nature; never be in frontal opposition, but learn to control it by swinging with it."

At precisely what point this inner essence of spirituality came to Lee, we can only guess.

In her book, *Bruce Lee: The Man Only I Knew*, his wife Linda recounts an incident which occurred after Ip Man had sent his young student home, ordering him not to train for seven days, but to use the time to meditate on the gentleness he could not seem to cultivate. The result was a high school essay in which Lee describes sudden insight into the nature of water while sailing along in a sampan. Had he perhaps perceived the living embodiment of advice to be found in the I-Ching?

"Under heaven, nothing is more soft and yielding than water. Yet for attacking the solid and strong, nothing is better; it has no equal. The weak can overcome the strong; the supple can overcome the stiff."

Legend tells us of Yen Hui, a student of Confucius, who one day went to his master and said; "I am making progress." "In what way?" asked Confucius. "I have given up doing good and being in the right," replied Yen Hui.

"That is very good, but not quite good enough." Some time later, Yen Jui approached Confucius and said again, I am making progress." And again, Confucius enquired of him, "In what way?"

"I just sit and forget," replied Yen Hui. Confucius was much taken aback, but nevertheless asked his student, "What do you mean by sitting and forgetting?"

"I am free of the body, and I have given up any idea of knowledge," replied Yen Hui, "By becoming free of body and mind, I can become one with the universe. This is what I mean by to sit and forget." Confucius thought for a moment. "When there is oneness," he said, "There can be no preferences. When there is change, there can be no constancy. If you have truly obtained this, then let me become your pupil."

Rather though than this sort of flashing insight, the achievement of inner harmony of this young martial artist was more of a gradual process, achieved as much through the bond that he developed with Ip Man, a bond that can only be forged through the sharing of the hardships and disciplines of martial arts training, and that can only be truly under-

Again, Lee has to parry a right punch, this time to the body. He uses a middle line inside block with the knife hand, although contact is always made using the hard outside of the forearm, in this case to the inside of the forearm. Lee is in the cat stance, 70% of the body weight on the rear leg. Moving forward, he brings his rear hand down onto the blocked arm, using the palm heel to smash his opponent's arm downwards, leaving his face exposed to a spear thrust with the leading arm. Using a left handed punch this time, Dan Inosanto again finds it blocked with a middle line inside block using the palm heel. Note that Lee's wrist and fingers are always tightly tensed when using this particular technique. Lee then moves in to finish the fight with a leading front kick using the ball of the foot to either face, abdomen or groin.

In a more lighthearted vein, Bruce Lee takes the role of attack and invites his student to play the part of defender. Inosanto uses a left-handed block, stepping inside Lee's right handed punch. He then delivers a back-handed knife hand blow to the unprotected stomach. At this point, both men find it all a little too much, and the demonstration develops into one of horse play. Inosanto tries to catch Bruce with a half-hearted hook kick. "What was that?" asks Lee.

stood by those who tread the way of the martial arts. It was a bond that was to last until the death of the old master in 1973.

Professor Ip would have approved of Bruce Lee's legacy though, for despite the fact that Lee was to outlive him by merely a few months, his life, and his death, were to act as a catalyst to the martial arts, particularly to Jeet Kune Do and Wing Chun, bringing their philosophies and techniques to a much wider audience than would otherwise have been possible.

Ip Man had taught Lee well, for in the coming year, he was to pursue philosophy and spirituality in a lifelong quest for self knowledge and personal expression, and through years of study of all forms of physical training, martial arts and fighting techniques, to develop a totally new concept of the martial arts.

By 1958 though, Lee had learned all he could from Ip Man, and against a background of brawling and serious rifts with other street youngsters, Lee was packed off to America by his parents for a change of environment.

Bruce Lee's early days in America and his later sojourn at Seattle University have been well catalogued, and it is beyond the scope of this book to go far into them here. Suffice it to say that insofar as examining what effect these times were to have on his art, the reverse more probably applies, and that it was Kung Fu which was inevitably to shape the events of Bruce Lee's later life. The fusing of the two elements of philosophy and pure martial technique were to reach their culmination in the Tao of Jeet Kune Do, published

This is the first of two line forms or katas, demonstrated by Lee in this book. The first shown here is a simple straight line form, using cat and horse stances. Although Lee did not believe too much in formal exercises, in his knowledge and practice of them, he was second to none. Lee starts in the cat stance. His leading arm is bent at 45°, the hand in the tiger-claw position, ready to attack. The rear hand, also in the tiger-claw position is held horizontally across the abdomen ready to defend or counter attack. Lee steps through with his left leg and turns his hips through 90° to place him in a left handed version of the previous stance. Stepping through again, this time with his right leg, Lee reverses the hand positions again but steps into a horse stance, at 45° to the front, performing a downward block with the right wrist, turning the hand and fingers well in, and following with a spear stab using the left hand. From the horse stance,

on which the weight is evenly distributed on both legs, Bruce twists his hips to the front, and drops 70% on his weight onto his front leg, straightening his back leg. This is the forward leaning stance, and from here, he stabs with a right handed spear thrust, in the high line. Stepping through in the final movement of this form with his left leg, he goes once again into the cat stance, executing a reverse thrust with his rear hand in the spear position. The form over, Lee relaxes, reflecting perhaps on his performance for the camera.

posthumously by his wife, Linda. Above all, Lee considered himself a martial artist first and an actor second. The acting was however, to come later.

During his early life in America, Lee practiced voraciously, examining other styles and forms of combat for what they had to offer, and in the process amassing a phenomenal library of the martial arts, over 2,000 volumes. The result of this constant reappraisal and collection was to be Jeet Kune Do, not so much another style, but one unique individual's way of thinking and approach to the martial arts.

"A good cook changes his knife but once a year, for he cuts," wrote Chuang Tsu in his Seven Chapters, "while a mediocre cook has to change his knife every month because he hacks. There are spaces between the joints, and the knife has no thickness. That which has no thickness has infinite room to pass through these spaces. Thus, after nineteen years, my blade is as sharp as ever."

Lee's rejection of the mediocrities and limitations of classical styles was not merely another example of empty arrogance. No one can dispute his massive ego, which was to blossom under the constant adulation that he was to receive as an international film star, but Lee was not merely a five-minute wonder. He often scoffed in public at the classical forms, or katas performed by other styles of Kung Fu and Karate. But he, better than most, realised that many of the different styles had much to offer, but that the potential was merely being strangled by an over emphasis on the traditional form.

He did not merely brush aside the classical approach however, but was to analyse it, see its faults, and thereby try to learn a lesson from it.

Critics of Lee and his philosophies and technique would therefore do well to remember that Jeet Kune Do was only a result of years of mastery of classical forms and styles, and that Lee undoubtedly knew far more about all the myriad forms of combat - both armed and unarmed, than those who sought to tear him down.

One reason that Lee was so openly scornful of many martial arts, particularly those of Karate and Japanese extraction was the traditional animosity between Japan and China on the attempts of many exponents of Karate and Bushido to deny the Chinese origins of their art. Much of this dates from a (relatively) recent meeting in 1936 of Okinawan karate masters, sponsored by an Okinawan newspaper. It is generally accepted that the Ryukyu Islands and Okinawa formed the bridge across which Kung Fu was to find its way to Japan from China, via groups of Chinese settlers (the 'thirty families') in the fourteenth century. In Japanese, the ideograms for Karate comprise two Chinese characters, Kara, or in Chinese T'ang, and Te or Shou. Kara indicated that it is of Chinese origin, specifically referring to the T'ang dynasty (618-960 A.D.), known as the Age of Enlightenment.

At the 1938 meeting, the decision was made to alter the ideogram for Kara in order to erase the Chinese connections for political reasons. In its place was the ideogram also pronounced 'Kara,' but in this case meaning 'empty' substituted, giving the present representation of Karate as 'empty hand.'

Manifestations of this chauvinistic feeling echo very strongly in Lee's second film, Fist of Fury, (American title The Chinese Connection) which involve a bloody and slaughterous feud with a Japanese Karate school. Exponents of the Japanese school enter Lee's Kung Fu institute in Shanghai (at that time under Japanese dominance) during the funeral of the school's master, and insult Lee and his fellow students, taunting them by calling them (the Chinese) the 'sick men of Asia.' The rest of the film is devoted to showing us that in fact the

Chinese are just the opposite, and are in fact superior in the martial arts to the Japanese.

There are notable exceptions of course, among attempts by the Japanese to deny the true origins of their art. Masutatsu Oyama, probably the greatest living karate master, and founder of the Kyokushinkai School in Tokyo teaches that karate derives much from Kenpo (Ch'uan Fa), and teaches many of the original techniques to his followers. Doshin So, another Japanese master, and founder of the Shorinji Kempo (Shaolin boxing) school on the island of Shikoku, spent many years in China before the Second World War, studying the scattered remnants of Kempo (Ch'uan Fa) in order to systemise and teach it in as near as possible its original style.

How then, did Jeet Kune Do develop? Most obviously, it has its roots in Wing Chun Kung Fu, which Lee continued to teach for several years after his arrival in America. In a Seattle basement he opened his first school - the Jun Fan Gung Fu Institute - 'Bruce Lee's Kung Fu Institute' - in an attempt to support himself and his then new wife, Linda.

It was during this period, and their subsequent move to California that Jeet Kune Do began to develop. Like Madame Yim Wing Chun before him, Lee began to feel the restriction of style, and that somehow he had to alter his way of fighting.

To change his style, Lee began to throw in everything he had learned, and what he was also constantly learning, and then began to eliminate everything that was not practical, hacking away inessentials, giving rise to the 'daily decrease' doctrine that he imparted to his students. This 'daily decrease' in technique, the removal of restrictions and complications was constantly going on right up until his death. As fiercely as he was critical of others, he was even more critical of himself.

Even as he tried to include techniques under such headings as strikes, blocks, and immobilisations, he would realise that one particular heading was too restrictive or inadequate, and that it could be applied to other techniques as well, and would start the process all over again in a constant reappraisal.

In as much as the number and type of strikes and blocks is itself limited by the nature of the human body itself, what was it that made Jeet Kune Do more than merely an encyclopaedia of the fighting arts, or even an anthology of its best features? The answer lies very much in the embodiment of Jeet Kune Do in its creator. For many of us, the two remain inseparable. In the following chapter we shall discuss the future of Jeet Kune Do, but it remains to be seen where the path of this particular martial art will lead now that its mentor has gone.

The basic underlying principle of the Martial Art, under whatever title it might go, is however one of pure physics. Simply, it is the total concentration of power at the instant and location of the strike, and is arrived at by the following equation: EMv^2 - where E is the Energy, or power of the blow, M is Mass, or the amount of muscle power put into the strike, and v is the Velocity, or speed at which the blow is delivered. Thus:

Power of the Blow Proportional Mass x The Square of the Velocity.

This gives us some insight into the devastating power of Lee's techniques. His legendary speed we have already discussed, however, it should be borne in mind that the power of the blow is inversely proportional to the time it takes to reach its target. For Lee, although possessed of sufficient muscle power to make his kicks and punches effective, was not muscle bound like many of the champions he was to encounter, and still had the phenomenal speed which was necessary to make him virtually unstoppable. He knew

almost instinctively that the key to all of the techniques was the speed and effective use of strength, rather than the emphasis placed on strength alone by many of the 'hard' systems.

Bruce Lee had taken what he needed from Wing Chun, and to it had added whatever he thought effective from other styles. His catalogue of Jeet Kune Do 'tools' reads like a 'Who's Who' of every form - of unarmed combat - from a simple straight leading punch to a head butt, or wrestling stranglehold!

The unique difference came in the philosophy of the application of these 'tools' however. Just because the student knew all these techniques and weapons of the body, he should not be tied by feeling obligated to use all of them, or even any of them. Flowing freely in a combat situation, the student should feel instinctively which technique to use at the right moment.

"The way of combat is not based on personal choice and fancies. Truth in the way of combat is perceived from moment to moment, and only when there is awareness without condemnation, justification, or any form of identification."

Fitness was an important part of Lee's method, one that he believed was neglected in the constant striving for perfection of skill and technique. Not that any one element should be neglected in favour of another, for both physical condition and fighting expertise are essential to win in a real fight. Lee's physical condition was a shining example to all his students. Standing at 5'7," and weighing in at about 140 pounds, his body was tuned to peak efficiency and endurance.

Lee's philosophy of physical fitness was much akin to that of Jeet Kune Do - to chisel away all that was superfluous, making his body a fighting machine capable of delivering a blow of the maximum power in the minimum of time.

Lee's daily workout included a four mile run, three quarters of an hour on a training cycle, skipping, shadow boxing, and sparring with an actual opponent.

Sparring, or free-fighting was the actual heart of real combat training for Jeet Kune Do students, Here, the student was faced with an unpredictable moving opponent who could hit back. Up to a point, practicing techniques singly or even in groups is fine as a method of training, building power and speed into the movements, but without sparring, or practice fighting. Kung Fu for one person is no more than a game.

After examining stances of various styles, such as the Horse stance of classical Kung Fu and the cat stance. Bruce Lee was to develop one for actual combat, which he was to call simply the 'On-guard Position,' which he used as a foundation on which to build the techniques. The on guard position is a semi-crouch stance, perfect for actual combat, as it provides the body with complete ease and relaxation, comfortably placed for both attack and defence, ready for either small steps for speed and controlled balance or for long lunging hook and side kicks.

The on-guard position is also perfect for mobility and fluidity in motion, a reflection on Lee's insistence that the fighter must at all times remain loose and relaxed. It creates an illusion of 'poker body' to the opponent, much like the 'poker face' concealing your intended movements. The fighter should adopt the stance with the stronger hand and foot forward, as these will do eighty per cent of the work.

From the on guard position, which embodies most of what is excellent within Jeet Kune Do as a combat method - good balance, swift attack and defence, and above all

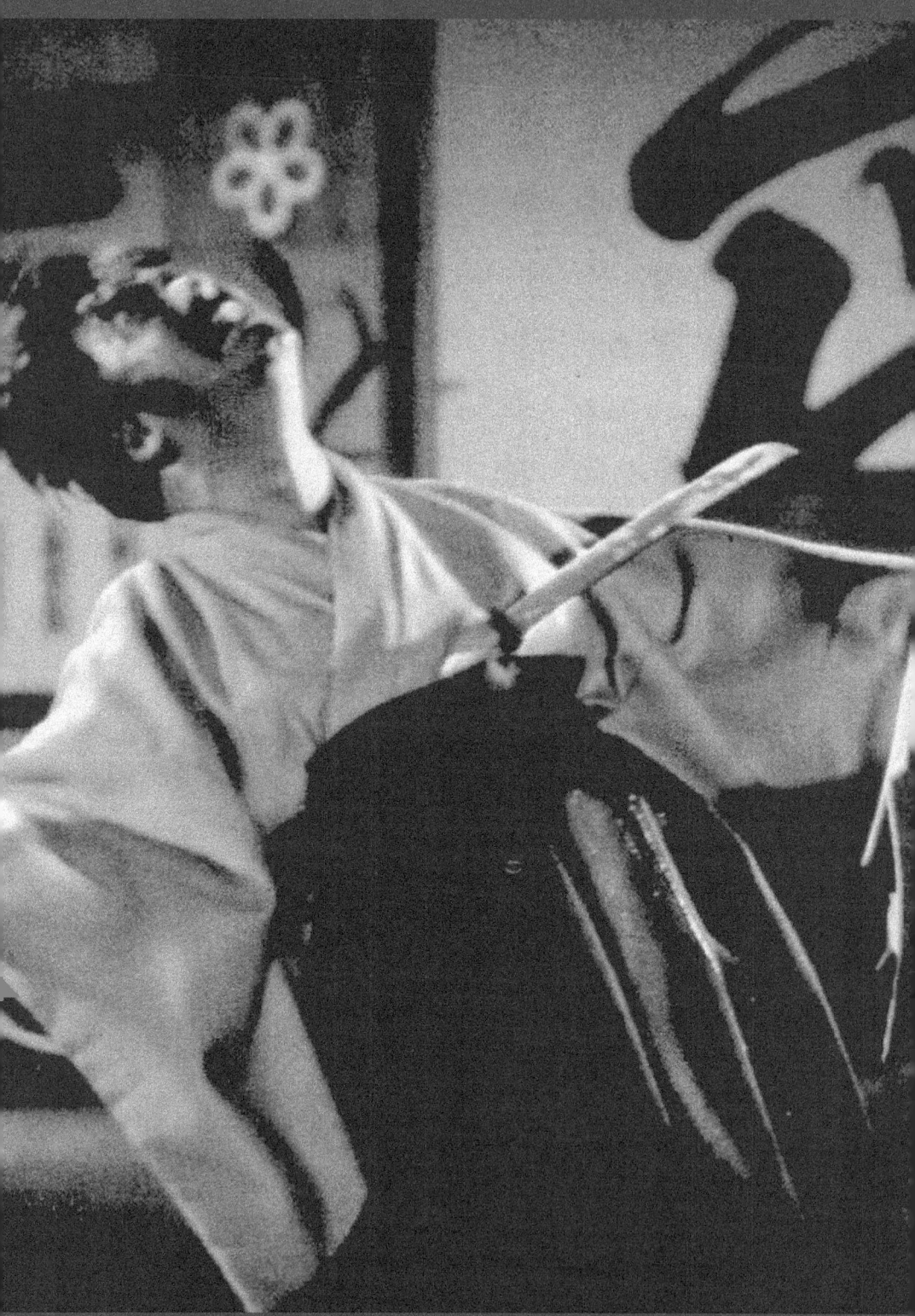

readiness to respond to any situation, all of the techniques could be performed. At this point, your attention is again drawn to the photographs contained throughout this book and their accompanying explanatory text. Together they form an essential part of this examination of the art of Bruce Lee.

To examine each of the Little Dragon's techniques, to ponder its origins, and to compare it with the classical style would be a lifetime's work.

However, to conclude this section, let us take two of Lee's favourite deliveries, the leading straight punch, and the leading side-kick, and examine them individually and compared with the classical approach.

The leading straight right punch, launched from the on guard position, is the 'bread and butter' punch of Jeet Kune Do, supremely effective because of its short, accurate and speedy delivery. Contrary to popular belief, the punch or thrust is the most basic weapon in the arsenal of all the martial arts, and not the popularised 'chop' or knife-hand blow. In the classical system of Kung Fu and Karate, the punch (Seiken Chudan Tsuki in Japanese) is initiated from the hip or midriff in a square-on stance, sanchin (pigeon toed) stance, or horse stance. The withdrawn fist, which performs the punch, is held back at the waist or chest (depending on the style), while the opposite hand is held in a forward position. As the punching fist is driven forwards, the fist turns from an upwards position to face palm downwards at the moment of impact. The punch is made with the first two knuckles of the fist. Simultaneously, the forward arm is drawn sharply back to create a 'counter force,' and ends in the same position in which the punching fist started, palm upwards at the waist. The immediate disadvantage of this system is that it leaves one half of the body open to attack.

In comparison, the Jeet Kune Do delivery is launched from the on guard position with the leading hand, and is delivered with a straight trajectory at the opponent's head.

One of the major advantages of the Jeet Kune Do punch, despite the fact that you are still well covered with your rear hand, which does not move, is that it can reach its target much quicker than that of the classical stylist, because of the shorter distance it has to travel. The punch is also thrown with the fist held vertically, which affords the attacker an extra three inches reach, which can be vital. The guarding hand is held high to protect the upper body from counter attack, acting as a supplement to the other hand, in a tactical position for a follow up.

The leading straight right however, is not just a 'flick.' Delivering the punch in a straight line, aligned with the lead foot and a properly balanced body, uses this section of the body as an axis to generate power. The straight punch is not an end, but a means towards an end, in that, although it will not floor an opponent, it is the key punch in Jeet Kune Do, and is used extensively in combinations of kicks and punches.

Bruce Lee taught that it was no good to punch 'soft' however. It common with most of leading forms of martial art, the leading straight right punch is not executed using the muscles of the arm alone. As we have already seen, the effectiveness of any strike depends on the degree of efficient muscle power behind the delivery, in other words, using the whole body as a weapon. Initially, the power originates in the hips and diaphragm, and by utilisation of precise coordination is transmitted through the torso, shoulder and wrist to the fist at the instant of contact. By turning the wrist slightly downwards before delivery and straightening it upon impact a twisting effect can be added to the opponent.

Bruce Lee with one of his translations of an ancient Chinese poem. Lee was a philosopher as much as a master of the martial arts, and an avid student of ancient writings, which he believed held much significance for us in today's world.

Lee also impressed on his students the desirability of ending the punch with a snap several inches behind the target, punching through an opponent rather than at him, a technique which will be familiar to those who practice 'tameshiwari' or breaking techniques.

The second of Lee's favourite attacks is the leading side kick, itself the single most powerful weapon in the Jeet Kune Do arsenal.

Even if successfully blocked, and this would take a highly competent fighter, its power is such that it will still succeed in hurting or staggering an opponent. A kick has two major advantages over a punch. Firstly, because the leg is much stronger than the arm, it is immensely more powerful. Secondly, as the leg is longer than the arm, it can be delivered from a greater distance, and is very difficult to block in the low line, particularly in such areas as the shin, knee, and groin.

Because of this greater reach however, and the fact that the attacker is standing on one leg while performing the kick, it is dangerous to attack with the feet unless it can be done with good balance and great speed.

The leading side-kick was Bruce Lee's speciality, demonstrated amply in his four major starring movies, but it differs considerably from the classical side-kick. A side snap-kick in traditional forms has the necessary speed, but lacks real power, while the side stamp-kick, using the heel, or edge of the foot, has the power lacking in the former, but not the speed.

In the Jeet Kune Do version, the best elements of both are present, so it retains the speed without loss of power by the simple expedient of twisting the hips just an instant before the leg reaches its full extension.

The foot is lifted twelve inches from the ground and is stamped straight outwards, keeping the knee of the supporting slightly bent to maintain balance, and pivoting on the ball of the foot as you thrust with the kicking leg. By adding a snap to the foot at the moment of full extension, devastating power can be added to the twisting effect of swivelling the hips.

When demonstrating this kick, Bruce Lee could drop a two-inch thick board from shoulder height and shatter it in half in mid air before it could reach the ground - an indication of the almost incredible speed and power of both man and technique.

Like the sting of a snake, the fast kick should be felt and not seen.

THE UNBEATABLE BRUCE LEE

With total mastery of style and form, Bruce Lee demonstrates Siu Lim Tao, one of the more complex forms of Wing Chun King Fu. In this form, the feet do not move, except at the end, and the entire kata is one of complex hand and wrist movements derived from the 'sticking hands' technique. The form is performed in the pigeon-toed stance, which although somewhat unaesthetic to the viewer is nevertheless eminently practical as a means of building great strength in the legs and diaphragm. The feet are turned inwards at 45°, shoulder-width apart, knees bend, both legs tensing tightly inwards, with the muscles of the buttocks and diaphragm also tensed. The toes of the rear foot are in line with the heel of the forward foot. Lee performs a double thrust to the face, using the first two knuckles of the fist. He brings his arms sharply back crossed at the throat in the knife hand, to break an opponent's stranglehold. Immediately both hands are thrust back out in a double spear-hand thrust, followed by a double palm-heel thrust to the chin. The hands are dropped to cover against attack to the groin. In kata, all movements are performed as if against an imaginary attacker, although obviously not designed to meet a set combat situation in this sequence, but rather as a means of developing muscular tension and familiarity with the techniques and their fluid combination. The right hand is withdrawn as a fist to the side of the chest, while Lee performs a middle line block or parry with the palm heel of the left hand. From this position, he uses the same hand to execute a wrist block in the left high line. The left hand is then withdrawn to the chest, and a right handed spear thrust made to the opponent's solar plexus, with the arm kept bent at 45°. Using the same arm, Lee forms a fist, and without withdrawing his hand, snaps it to full extension in a right handed punch to the head. The fist is then driven downwards in a hammer blow or block before being withdrawn to the chest as the left hand performs an inside mid-

dle-line parry using the inside edge of the forearm. The photographs shows a sequence of wrist techniques used for blocking, striking, and breaking an opponent's hold on the clothing of the arms and body. From a circular break of a grip on the sleeve, Lee turns his opponent's arm inwards against the joint, and immediately using the same arm to make a finger strike to the eyes. The right hand is then

withdrawn as in picture, and both arms simultaneously thrust forward in a crossed-arm block. The arms are crossed at the wrist, forming a solid crotch in which a kick or punch can be stopped dead. It is extremely important here, to tense both wrists and hands, as rather than a parry, which merely deflects the force of an opponent's blow, the crossed arm block meets the attack head on, absorbing

all its force. From this position, Bruce executes a right leading punch, raising his rear arm to a defensive position across the chest. In the final movement of this form, he now brings his feet together into the ready stance, and executes the roundhouse block of Chinese Kenpo. The basis of the roundhouse block, one of the fundamental techniques of Kenpo, can best be described by likening it to the whirl-

ing blades of a fan. Although when the blades of the fan are stationary, an object may easily pass between them, when the fan is set in motion, no object can pass through them without obstruction. The roundhouse block, a circular movement with both hands moving in opposite directions on the circumference of a circle, uses this principle to deflect and trap an opponent's attack. Finally, Bruce

turns both palms downwards at the completion of the block and exhales through the nose, ending the kata in this position.

THE KUNG-FU MONTHLY ARCHIVE SERIES

In these six photographs, Bruce Lee demonstrates some of the movements of Tai Chi-Chuan, the Chinese system of healthy calisthetics. The first photographs show 'Chasing the Wind.' In the last photographs, Lee demonstrates the 'Golden Rooster Standing on One Leg.' These exercises are designed as a series of bodily calisthetics, and have little real connection with the martial arts.

CHAPTER FOUR

JEET KUNE DO: THE WAY FORWARD

> "My sons, here is the wholesome teaching. Wisdom hidden - is wasted, is treasure that never sees the light of day. Silence is rightly used when it masks folly, not when it is the grave of wisdom."
>
> **ANCIENT CHINESE SCRIPTURE**

High above a Warchai Street, the red light district of Hong Kong, hangs a gigantic photograph enlargement of the Little Dragon, across which is written in Chinese characters the simple epitaph: "The Spirit of Bruce Lee lives on..."

"If men have no fear of death," wrote Lao Tsu, "Then it is of no avail to threaten them with dying."

Lee had no fear of dying; rather he regarded it as a liberation from yet another restriction - life itself.

This it was, on July 20th 1973, at the age of thirty two, the leading light of the Chinese martial arts was so suddenly extinguished. Or was it? Perhaps, as the epitaph would suggest, although the body has gone, the spirit still survives and Bruce Lee was indeed truly liberated?

It might seem cynical, but would nevertheless be unrealistic to assume that Lee's death and the nature of it, did not in many ways create as much attention and comment as his life, but this apart, the contribution that he made to the martial arts remains unchanged.

How good was Bruce Lee? A question he revealed once on Hong Kong radio, that he was constantly asked. "I say, 'Well, if I tell you I'm good, probably you'll say I'm boasting. But if I tell you I'm no good, you will know I'm lying.'"

Certainly, his speed was phenomenal, setting him apart from other martial artists. And Lee was never beaten in his life, a considerable achievement when one considers the number of challenges which inevitably came his way.

Lee's belief in the superiority of his fluid style and speed was total, and posterity has proved him right. A testament to how good he really was can be seen by reading through a list of credits of guest martial artists in his films, who were happy to step forward and have Lee publicly pound them to the floor on celluloid.

Although it is largely pointless to ask whether Bruce Lee could have beaten other contemporary masters of different styles, for each is an undisputed expert in their own field, it is this author's opinion that when it really matters perhaps, in a no holds barred street fight, Bruce Lee could have beaten anyone in the world.

But Jeet Kune Do, Bruce Lee's legacy to both those who loved and followed him, and to the world of the martial arts, was much more than a supremely efficient method of street fighting or of beating up an opponent. Bruce Lee spent twenty years studying, refining, changing and finally leading forward his art, most of his lifetime in fact, and the least that even his hardest critics can do is to take him seriously. The hardships endured, and the self discipline and sheer will power needed to survive the 'way' of the martial arts cannot properly be comprehended by the outsider.

But other Kung Fu and Karate masters have devoted much of their lives to the development of their own particular styles, so what was it that made Jeet Kune Do so different?

Simply, Jeet Kune Do is the first totally complete combat system developed for the needs of the modern man. Although not completely eschewing its roots in the classical styles and philosophies of Zen, it is nevertheless built on a firm foundation of practicality, with one basic underlying precept - that the object of any fighting method is ultimately to survive, which means beating the opponent at any cost.

Jeet Kune Do is as much a way of thinking as a technique or collection of techniques, and reposes in the mind of its practitioner as his physical skills.

"Adapt or die," was one of Lee's doctrines. But where does Jeet Kune Do go from here,

now that its creator has left us? Now that the master has gone, will the art still continue to refine and change?

Although only time will tell, much now rests with Lee's former students, in particular those closest to him, to whom he imparted much of his wisdom and technique.

Karate and the Japanese martial arts notwithstanding, Kung Fu and Jeet Kune Do has been Bruce Lee's revolution. His supreme ability, and his confidence in himself - the two inseparable - have formed an example for countless numbers of us.

"If we know our opponent, and if we know ourselves, there will be no fear in a hundred battles," the Sun-Tsu tells us, "If we do not know our opponent, but we know our-

selves, the odds are even. But if we know neither the opponent nor ourselves, then there is danger in a hundred battles."

Lee believed that self-knowledge was the touchstone of Jeet Kune Do, therein laying its effectiveness. The learning of Jeet Kune Do is not merely the accumulation of stylised technique, but rather the understanding of the root of ignorance.

Surely, with the millions awed by his cinematic feats, and through the countless thousands of martial arts students who he inspired with his spirit, teachings, and unique brand of fighting, the Way of the Intercepting Fist will continue to live on...

Bruce Lee in seated Zazen, or Zen meditation.

THE UNBEATABLE BRUCE LEE

Bruce Lee relaxes amongst his many volumes of books covering every form of the martial arts. Lee was a voracious reader, constantly on the lookout for new ideas and techniques, and during his lifetime was to amass a library of over 2,000 books on every aspect of the unarmed arts. Note the pair of nunchaku hanging from the centre of the bookcase.

ALSO BY THE AUTHOR

THE K.F.M. BRUCE LEE SOCIETY

"BEAUTIFULLY CAPTURES THE HEART, SOUL, AND SPIRIT OF THE UNITED KINGDOM'S FLEDGLING BRUCE LEE FANBASE. UNDENIABLY COLLECTIBLE."

- BRUCE LEE REVIEW

"NOT JUST A COMPILATION OF NOSTALGIC NEWSLETTERS, BUT A BRITISH HISTORY GUIDE TO A PERIOD TIME WHEN WESTERN PEOPLE DISCOVERED THE UNIQUE TALENTS OF THE UN-DISPUTED KING OF KUNG FU - BRUCE LEE."

- ANDREW J. STATON, BRITISH JUN FAN JOURNAL

"THANK YOU VERY MUCH FOR YOUR TIME AND EFFORT TO HONOUR PAM FOR HER GREAT WORK AND DEDICATION. I, TOGETHER WITH THE BRUCE LEE FANS WHO KNEW PAM SALUTE YOU!"

- ROBERT LEE

THE **KUNG-FU MONTHLY** BRUCE LEE SECRET SOCIETY BEGAN IN SEPTEMBER 1976, RUNNING FOR 30 ISSUES BEFORE IT'S FINAL ISSUE IN SEPTEMBER 1983. RUN BY THE FORMIDABLE PAM HADDEN, THE BRUCE LEE SECRET SOCIETY FUNCTIONED AS THE SOURCE OF INFORMATION FOR BRUCE LEE FANS IN THE UK AND LATER, THE REST OF THE WORLD. FOR THE FIRST TIME EVER, ALL 30 ISSUES HAVE BEEN PAINSTAKINGLY RE-EDITED AND RE-PRINTED IN THIS BOOK, ALONG WITH UPDATED NOTES AND RETROSPECTIVE STORIES BY THE PEOPLE MOST RESPONSIBLE FOR KEEPING BRUCE LEE'S MEMORY ALIVE - THE FANS.

AVAILABLE FROM **WWW.KUNGFUMONTHLY.UK & AMAZON**

THE WORLD FAMOUS
MARKETPLACE

DON'T FORGET TO VISIT OUR WEBSITE FOR OTHER FANTASTIC ITEMS INCLUDING CLOTHING AND LIMITED EDITION SETS!

◀ BRUCE LEE
KING OF KUNG FU

Written by Felix Dennis & Don Atyeo, Bruce Lee King of Kung Fu is the original and still one of the greatest books on Bruce Lee ever written. Packed with photos and essential information from the immediate year after Lee's tragic death, Bruce Lee King of Kung Fu provides the best of rock-solid backgrounds to the story of the man we all know and love.
170 PAGES

BUY ONLINE NOW!
amazon
WHSmith
Waterstones
OR VISIT OUR WEBSITE AT
WWW.KUNGFUMONTHLY.UK

KUNG-FU MONTHLY ▶
THE POSTER MAGAZINES

Volume One - No. 1 to 25, trade dummy plus an in-depth article on The History of Kung-Fu Monthly 1973 to 1979.
Volume Two - No. 26 to 55 plus interviews with former KFM staff.
Volume Three - No. 56 to 79, double-poster special edition issue plus an in-depth article on The History of Kung-Fu Monthly 1980 to 1984.
540-670 PAGES

THE BOOK OF ▶
KUNG-FU

The Book of Kung Fu was to be Kung-Fu Monthly's special annual issue, but was only published in 1974. Over one-hundred pages, many of them in colour, with a durable soft cover and scores of photographs, illustrations and articles. Don't miss this book! Bruce Lee, Angela Mao, David Carradine, Kung Fu Quiz, Comic Book and more - an incredible publication!
144 PAGES

THE SECRET ART OF ▶
BRUCE LEE

THE KUNG FU MONTHLY ARCHIVE

In 1976, the world took its first look at the now legendary Chester Maydole photographs. Arranged where possible, in 'fast-frame' action sequences, The Secret Art of Bruce Lee shows the founder of Jeet Kune Do, assisted by his friend and student Dan Inosanto, demonstrating the early development state of his art Jeet Kune Do during early days in Los Angeles.
110 PAGES

THE LOST KFM BOOK
FIRST TIME EVER IN THE UK!

◀ **THE WISDOM OF BRUCE LEE**

The Wisdom of Bruce Lee was to be one of the first books in the world to look at Bruce Lee's philosophy on life and martial arts. Mysteriously never released in the UK, The Wisdom of Bruce Lee is finally available to UK Bruce Lee fans after a wait of over forty years.
The full-length version includes a new introduction and interview with author Roger Hutchinson by Jun Fan Journal writer Andrew Staton, while the shorter abridged version is formatted in the style of the original Kung-Fu Monthly books.
70 PAGES / 170 PAGES

◀ **THE UNBEATABLE BRUCE LEE**

The Unbeatable Bruce Lee presents readers with a fighter's view of Bruce Lee the man and Bruce Lee the martial arts master. Beneath the sheer weight of known facts and figures that surround the tragically short life of Hong Kong's number one son, lies a strata of truth that only now is beginning to be picked.
112 PAGES

◀ **BRUCE LEE IN ACTION**

With Bruce Lee in Action, the Editors of Kung-Fu Monthly had compiled another fine addition to their library of Bruce Lee publications. Lavishly illustrated throughout with many previously unseen photographs at the time, this informative book investigates clearly and concisely, the birth and subsequent development of Lee's fighting style Jeet Kune Do, both on and off the screen.
106 PAGES

THE POWER OF ▶ BRUCE LEE

Bruce Lee was possibly the greatest exponent of the martial arts ever produced. The fact that he was a movie star often clouds his enormous contribution to the field. The Power of Bruce Lee explores many of his revolutionary methods of attack and defence, especially those relating to Jeet Kune Do, Lee's name for his own fighting system
110 PAGES

WHO KILLED ▶ BRUCE LEE?

Who Killed Bruce Lee? is a study of the pressures and the forces that, on the one hand were to elevate him to the highest plains of stardom and on the other, were to so tragically strike him down before his final fulfilment.
Who Killed Bruce Lee? was one of the first books to delve deep into the newspaper stories of Lee's early death.
108 PAGES

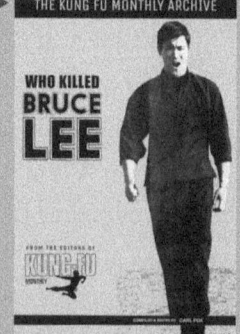

◀ **THE GAME OF DEATH**

This book combines two Kung-Fu Monthly special edition magazines released prior to Golden Harvest's 1978 film. Researched exclusively in Hong Kong, Kung-Fu Monthly reports on Lee's plot for Game of Death, the cast he intended to appear in the film, the scenes already filmed and Lee's hopes and expectations for the success of the project. Incredibly accurate for the time, this publication represents an important part of Bruce Lee fandom in the UK.
XXX PAGES

FIND OUT MORE INFORMATION AT

THE MAGAZINES

WWW.KUNGFUMONTHLY.UK

◀ **THE BEGINNER'S GUIDE TO KUNG FU**

Originally released in 1974, The Beginner's Guide to Kung Fu was the first martial arts book aimed primarily at the Kung Fu Craze generation. The graphic, easy to understand illustrations by Paul Simmons and the carefully conceived step by step instructions made this the perfect book for beginners who wished to take up Kung Fu.
XXX PAGES

▲
THE BRUCE LEE SCRAPBOOK
In 1974, Kung-Fu Monthly issued a Bruce Lee scrapbook in the form of a large A3 magazine, followed by a smaller A4 sized book in 1979. As part of the KFM Archive Series, both scrapbooks have been combined in a new chronological layout with brand new captions, location information and dates by Carl Fox and Jun Fan Journal writer Andrew Staton.
150 PAGES

THE KFM BRUCE LEE SOCIETY ▶

Long before the internet communities we know today, The Bruce Lee Society was the source of information in the United Kingdom for all things Bruce Lee. Now the history of the Bruce Lee Society is finally told in The Bruce Lee Society: A Retrospective Look at Bruce Lee Mania and the Kung Fu Craze of the 1970s. For the first time ever, all thirty issues of The Bruce Lee Society newsletters have been painstakingly re-edited and re-printed in this book, along with updated notes and retrospective stories by the people most responsible for keeping Bruce Lee's memory alive - the fans.
544 PAGES

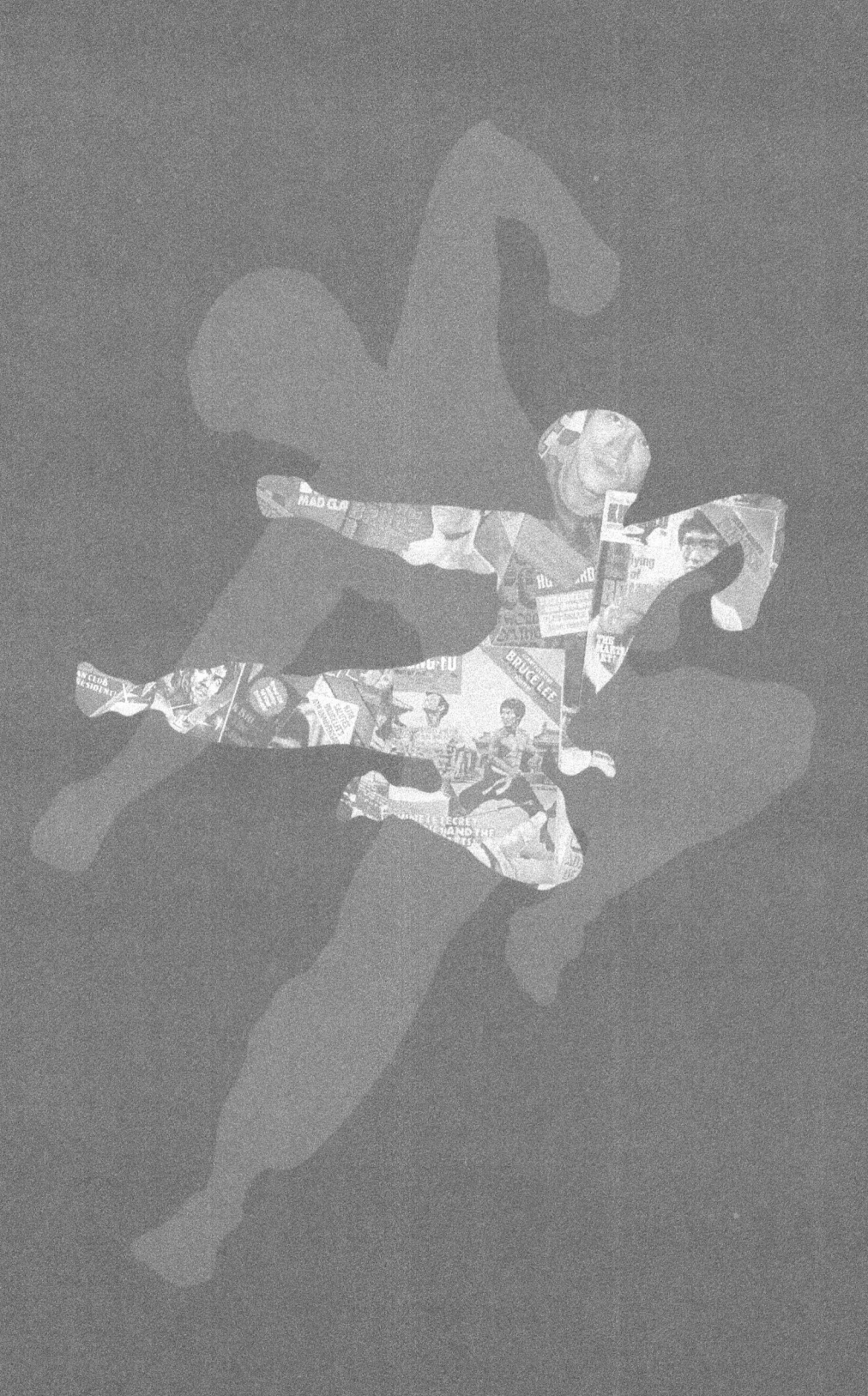

www.ingramcontent.com/pod-product-compliance
Lightning Source LLC
Chambersburg PA
CBHW041322110526
44591CB00021B/2882